Walking by the River

100 NEW HYMN AND SONG TEXTS 1998–2008,

WITH OTHER VERSES,

BY CHRISTOPHER M IDLE

100 NEW HYMN AND SONG TEXTS 1998–2008,
WITH OTHER VERSES,
BY CHRISTOPHER M IDLE

THE GOOD BOOK COMPANY
HOPE PUBLISHING COMPANY

See permissions and copyrights on page xiii.

Published by
The Good Book Company
Elm House, 37 Elm Road
New Malden
Surrey KT3 4HN, UK
Tel: 0845-225-0880
Fax: 0845-225-0990
Email: admin@thegoodbook.co.uk
Internet: www.thegoodbook.co.uk

In association with
Hope Publishing Company
380 South Main Place
Carol Stream, IL 60188
USA

Unless indicated, all Scripture references are taken from the HOLY BIBLE,
NEW INTERNATIONAL VERSION. Copyright © 1973, 1978, 1984 International Bible Society.

ISBN: 978-1-906334-48-2

Cover design: Tim Thornborough
Author Photograph: Edmund Boyden

*Christopher Martin Idle, born in September 1938, spent 30 years in parish ministry in the Church of England in both urban and rural settings. His first hymn-collection, **Light upon the River**, marked his 60th birthday in 1998. The present book gathers the fruit of the ten years since then. In the decade of these hundred, their author has also written **Real Hymns, Real Hymn Books** (Grove, 2000) and **Exploring Praise vols 1 and 2** (Praise Trust 2006 and 2007, a companion to the hymn-book **Praise!**, 2000).*

*He has four married sons, and as grandchildren kept arriving in this period – eleven so far – **Grandpa's Amazing Poems and Awful Pictures** appeared in 2005 (with better illustrations by Howard Garbutt). Chris's wife Marjorie died in February 2003; in September that year he moved to Bromley and joined Holy Trinity Church, Bromley Common.*

CHRISTMAS, FROM A DISTANCE

And did he pass through Bethlehem
and pause a moment by the fold
to see the shepherds, watching them,
and notice some were getting old
but might remember, years ago,
that sudden brightness in the sky
and wonder, Was it really so?
Or was it like a dream gone by
to fade, like faith and hope and love?
And yet, there was a manger there,
the straw below, the sky above;
a tiny baby's glistening hair,
his screwed-up eyes and wrinkled face –
and what a moment to arrive
on such a night, in such a place!
But could that tiny scrap survive?
And would they see him at the gate
and come and lean against the wall
and try to recollect the date,
that night when Glory found them all?

CONTENTS

Introduction . . . . *ix*

Permissions and Copyrights . . . . *xiii*

Hymn texts and notes:

      Hymns through the Bible, including Psalms 15

      Local and special 101

Appendices 1–3: two extras, and some altered texts 123

Indexes:

      Scriptures: selected 127

      Themes: selected 131

      Tunes (alphabetical) 134

      Contemporary composers 135

      Hymn texts 136

O give thanks unto the Lord, and call upon his Name: tell the people what things he hath done.

O let your songs be of him, and praise him: and let your talking be of all his wondrous works.

Rejoice in his holy Name: let the heart of them rejoice that seek the Lord.

I will be glad and rejoice in thee: yea, my songs will I make of thy Name, O thou most Highest.
                                      Psalms 105 vv 1–3, and 9 v 2,
                                      Book of Common Prayer.

'For songs of Syon, Lord, my soul prepare.'
                    G R Woodward, after J Scheffler,
                            in *'How dazzling fair art thou,*
                                      my Life, my Light'.

Thanksgiving and praise to Jesus belongs;
he claims for his grace New Testament songs:
our Saviour and Lover in hymns we proclaim,
and all the world over rejoice in his name.
                                      Charles Wesley,
                                      Short Hymns on Select
                            Passages of the Holy Scriptures:
                                      on Isaiah 42 v 10.

INTRODUCTION

'It is especially noteworthy', said Ralph C Wood in 2003 (writing about *The Lord of the Rings* in *The Gospel according to Tolkien*, p36), 'that various members of the Company, especially the hobbits, repeatedly have recourse to poetry and song.' Yes, indeed; one of the great losses in the often brilliant film version. Wood is talking about the precious gift of language, and continues: 'Speech at its fullest stretch is found in rhyme and meter [he's American], in alliteration and assonance and consonance, as well as in many other poetic devices. When sung, poetry takes on even greater import, as it lifts words into the higher dimension of shared celebration or else plunges them into the depths of communal lament.'

Yes, yes, again – as in the Psalms, where the Hebrew devices are different but equally employed and enjoyed. When Ralph Wood goes on to say 'That the words of Tolkien's poems and songs are simple and the rhymes predictable counts nothing against them...' I want to say, No indeed, for this is not the least part of their art. It is the simplest songs which need most labour to get right; they have to work with unsophisticated singers without benefit of an army of musicians performing on stage. The trouble with some 'worship songs' from the 1970s onwards is not that they teach us to love songs too much, but too little. The real songs – evocative, imaginative, skilful, satisfying – have been all-but-engulfed by oceans of self-satisfied, unoriginal, and repetitive jingles.

By the year 2000 there were signs of improvement among the best song-writers, though much of the earlier output remained available in print and recordings. A congregation could be asked to sing half a dozen of such items without a mention of anything that God in Christ had actually done or said – or is doing or will do; it was all how I felt about it. Sometimes the name of the one addressed did not appear, so that 'I love you' (etc) could easily be interpreted by the casual visitor as a secular song to the human beloved.

In a seminar on hymn-writing I once led, 'song-writing' had somehow been added to my original topic. I did my best, putting on the screen some verses by Tolkien and some by the New Zealander Colin Gibson. It was their brilliant simplicity, vivid imagery and disciplined craft which, among other things, I pointed out. My chosen examples, I noted, were written by professors of

English; not that all academics have this gift, but these two clearly understood how language works at many levels. Their lyrics (for which, significantly, others provide the music) have a purposeful flow unhindered by awkward inversions or excess phrases; each word earns its place, and its place is the right one.

On that occasion I did not communicate well. In fact, I do not think that my students understood what I was talking about. Most of them seemed to go on writing what everyone else was writing, and too many congregations were expected to sing, at that time.

It may seem rash, after this, to introduce some song lyrics in this collection of hymns! But as in *Light upon the River* (1998) I venture to include a handful of items designed specifically for children. These come within the Bible order rather than as a separate category, partly since historically children's hymns have often proved popular with adults, and *vice versa*. Others in the song genre (through their specialised metres and specially-composed tunes) were usually requested for particular purposes, as the notes indicate. Unlike my earlier book, this collection places Psalm versions in their appropriate Scripture order; but the 'local' items again comprise a final section. Not all these are readily adaptable for more general use.

Now, this title; who exactly is 'walking by the river'? Specifically, it is our Lord Jesus Christ (John chapter 1) and many others there including, decisively, John the Baptist; nos. 42, 54 and especially 58 reflect this. The Lord also walked by the lake, the hills and the fields, in village, town and city. Walking today is an under-valued and much-to-be-recommended activity, for all kinds of reasons, and a familiar Biblical model of faith and discipleship from Noah and Enoch to Paul and John. For insights into walking in our car-crazed culture, see Peter Mortimer, *Broke Through Britain: One Man's Penniless Odyssey*, Mainstream Publishing 1999.

And rivers, from the Pishon and Tigris in Genesis to the water of life in Revelation. A river marks the title of my first collected volume and I find myself still writing about it, or rather them. Tolkien, A A Milne and Kenneth Grahame have some marvellous fictional rivers. Among real ones providing some great memories, accompanied by some of my dearest companions of whom Marjorie is the chief, are the Aln, Avon, Cam, Cherwell, Darenth, Duddon, Finnan, Great Ouse, Isis, Kelvin, Medway, Oberwater and the Weirs (Brockenhurst), Quaggy, Ravensbourne, Ruchugi (Tanzania), Tweed and Waveney. And many others – some more famous, some unnamed on the map, and two in a class of their own, Jordan and Thames.

In *Light upon the River* I paid tribute to several friends who had helped with words over the years, and I confirm my gratitude here. This time I also express my warm appreciation of all those musicians and composers who have in various ways encouraged, corrected, taught and helped me over the years – in some cases, decades. These include John Barnard, Gill Berry, John Crothers, Ruth Day, Sue Gilmurray (the finest Christian singer/songwriter of our time?), Anne Greenidge, Donald Hustad, David Iliff, Steve James, William Jones, Lyn Kendrick, Michael Lumgair, Linda Mawson, David Peacock, Brian Raynor, Agnes Tang, Noël Tredinnick, Norman Warren, David Wilson, Ruth Woodcraft; and the late Christopher Hayward (a multi-talented and irreplaceable friend and accomplice), Mervyn Horder, Howard Stringer and Donald Webster. Among other encouragers have been Brian, Deborah, John, Malcolm, Sally, Sara, Timothy, Wynne, another David and numerous Michaels. And many more of whom the best and most-missed was Marjorie, of whom I wrote more fully in 1998, little knowing how short would be our remaining time together. Every item up to September 2002 is all the better for her comments; I do not blame her for their shortcomings

It has been a rare privilege to remain in touch, not least through hymns, with a range of groups who do not always salute one another. That is, from Grace Baptists and FIEC enthusiasts to radical Christian pacifists and Scottish Presbyterians, from Hymn Society choirs and literary scholars to OMF and the Proclamation Trust; together with many shades of Anglican including Forward in Faith, even some musical bishops, and (where I am most naturally at home) the evangelical testimony borne by, for example, Crosslinks and Reform – not that even these two are co-terminous! But each of those named bears witness to truth and grace not always noticed by the rest; all have enriched my own thinking and writing.

Here the notes and indexing are simpler than in 1998; one reader implied that he did not need to know what I had for breakfast on the day I wrote a particular hymn. But one more address can be added to those given then as the main places of writing; on retirement I moved to a bungalow half way between the home I was born in (now demolished) and the source of the river Ravensbourne (still flowing) – address on the next page. This little book had several possible titles, but the rivers won in the end. The best earthly walks are often circular, while the crucial one has an eternal destination; let's enjoy both kinds, singing as we go! Psalm 23, as usual, says it all.

Christopher Idle,
Bromley, Kent 2008.

PERMISSIONS AND COPYRIGHTS

Some texts have been modified for a variety of reasons since they were first sung or printed; the version used here is the authorised text from the date of this publication. This also embodies the author's preferred style of layout, capitals, punctuation and spelling; there has to be some flexibility (e.g. for American readers or a publisher's house style), but such factors are designed chiefly for clarity of understanding and singing. Some may prefer the custom of representing the divine name, particularly in Psalm versions, by 'LORD' rather than 'Lord'; others opt for different spellings of 'Hallelujah'. If the suggested tune is not yet in print or readily available, a copy may usually be obtained from the author at 16 Cottage Avenue, Bromley, Kent BR2 8LQ, if a reply envelope is provided.

Copyright for all texts is held by the author and is administered, in the UK, by The Jubilate Group, c/o Paul Williams, 4 Thorne Park Road, Torquay TQ2 6RX, or e-mail: copyrightmanager@jubilate.co.uk; and in the USA by Hope Publishing Co, c/o Scott Shorney, 380 South Main Place, Carol Stream, IL 60188. For all other territories, please contact Jubilate Hymns for advice. Although in certain circumstances or one-off use fees may not be charged for copies, permission to use all texts should be sought from the appropriate administrator.

Members of the Christian Copyright Church or School Licensing Scheme may reproduce the words – applying the correct copyright ascription on each copy – and account for it in their annual CCL return. The texts are also available under CCLI, and some appear on the Jubilate or *Praise!* websites..

MYSTERY WORD?

Several references to TAG are not explained after no.2. This is the 'Text Advisory Group' of Jubilate Hymns, to which in its beginnings I belonged. It usually comprised three or four writers including at least one musician, who looked at hymn texts submitted by Jubilate Agency Members, to approve them (or not) for the website, and often made suggestions, major or minor, for improvement. As an author, I have found this sometimes painful but almost always immensely helpful.

HYMNS THROUGH THE BIBLE, INCLUDING PSALMS:

Some of these texts are intended as straight paraphrases; others are based on or illustrate one or more Scripture verses. Where several allusions are included, the hymns are arranged under a relevant or dominant verse while others may be traced through the Scripture Index.

HYMN TEXTS AND NOTES

Hymns through the Bible,
including Psalms

Genesis 1-3 etc.

Two ways to live (1: see no.13)

1 GOD, LOVING RULER OF OUR WORLD

God, loving ruler of our world,
all things were made by you;
by your creative, gracious power
you made us rulers too.

But we reject you; godless lives
spin out our sorry tale,
and in ourselves, our land, our world,
how hopelessly we fail!

You take us fairly at our word;
and if we still rebel
your judgement pays us what we ask:
the godless death of hell.

Yet you are love! You gave your Son;
this Man has met our need:
your rule he lived, our death he died,
the slaves of sin are freed!

You raised him from the stony grave,
to spell the end of death:
he brings good news, forgiveness, life:
he comes to judge the earth.

So grant me grace to follow Christ,
and I will surely pray,
trust all his words, accept his rule
and walk with him today.

CM   Tune: DUNFERMLINE, LONDON NEW, or BONNYTON by John Bell

Scriptures: Gen 1:26–31; 3   Deut 30:19–20   Luke 14:46–47   John 1:3; 8:34–36
Acts 17:30–31   Rom 1:18–25   2 Cor 5:14–21   1 John 4:8–16
Written: Peckham, Feb 1999; last stanza revised Bromley, May 2005.
Tim Thornborough of the Good Book Company, who have kindly taken me on again, suggested that a hymn could be based on the evangelistic outline 'Two Ways to Live'. With early help from Marjorie, here it is. We first sang it at Crinken, near Bray in the Irish republic, July 2000, as chosen from several options by the then vicar Gordon Fyles. In 2005 the ongoing editorial group of *Praise!* asked me to revise the concluding lines, and Linda Mawson suggested John Bell's tune.

Genesis 1:24–25; 2:19–20; 3:17 etc
God, Creator and Lord of insects

2 NOT EVEN ADAM GAVE A NAME

Not even Adam gave a name
to every insect there has been,
the myriad species in the frame
the naked eye has never seen:
      not only butterflies and bees
      or glinting wings of dragonflies,
      but creeping things in galaxies
      of less than microscopic size.

We marvel at one beetle's glow,
a moth half-hidden on a tree,
while far beyond our sight, we know,
their numbers touch infinity.
      The cycle of their death and birth,
      the food-chain and the parasite –
      their interwoven life on earth
      saves all that's green from endless night.

In hope of Eden's good restored
by our superb Creator-king
and marvellously skilful Lord
beyond all science, let us sing
      in faith to see that pledge fulfilled
      in Christ, on one amazing dawn,
      all poison cleansed, infection healed,
      unspoiled delight in worlds reborn.

LMD   Tune: FABRE, by John Crothers

Scriptures: Gen 1:24–25, 31; 2:19–20; 3:17 etc   Ps 148:10–13   Rom 8:19–21
Written: Bromley, Aug 2005: revised Nov 2005
First published: *Evangelicals Now* , March 2007

Beetles have delighted me from the age of 12. A recent statistic which I still need to read twice is that among the 350,000 known species are (for example) 35,000 different kinds of long-horned beetles. Insect species approach the million mark, with a possible further 9 million yet to be discovered. Yet most references to insects in hymns (Ryland, Toplady, Matheson etc) are something of a put-down! With the help of TAG (the Jubilate 'Text Advisory Group'; see pxiii) my original 4 stanzas shrank to 3, with the loss of some biblical locusts, ants and grasshoppers. John Crothers' tune was happily named by Timothy Dudley-Smith, after the French entomologist whose translated books I devoured from Bromley Library in my early teens.

Genesis 2–3

Two Adams

3 O ADAM, OUR ADAM, THE VERY FIRST MAN

O Adam, our Adam,
the very first man!
God spoke, and God made him
when all things began.
God gave him a garden
in Eden so fair;
and Eve at his side
for his love and his care.

O Adam, our Adam,
our Adam and Eve!
What God had commanded
they did not believe.
God said 'Do not do this',
but they said, 'We will';
and we do the same, and
we're doing it still.

But now a new Adam
has come on the scene,
for Jesus is greater than
all who have been.
We children of Adam
all need a new start,
and Jesus the Saviour
begins with our heart.

6565D Tune: ST DENIO

Scriptures: Gen 2–3   Acts 17:26   Rom 5:12–21   1 Cor 15:45–49
Written: Peckham, Jan 2001
The first of several school or 'All-age Service' songs in this collection, most (like this one)
written for Pilgrims' Way Primary School in the Old Kent Road. For some years I led weekly
assemblies for both Infants and Juniors (Key Stages 1 and 2) where such songs proved useful, words prominently displayed at the front while I led the singing from the piano. The im-
portance of Adam can hardly be over-stated; as the ancestor of the human family – one race
– he is both an antidote to the poisonous racism of rival ethnic groups, and also the contrasting or negative image of the 'Last Adam' who was to come. While not expecting children (or adults!) to grasp the full meaning of all the Bible texts, the song provides a basic
way in for understanding, and for faith.

Genesis 17:1–18:15 etc
For senior citizens

4   SINCE FIRST WE JOINED THE PILGRIM WAY

Since first we joined the pilgrim way
　to Zion's holy hill,
God's grace sustained us day by day;
through cloud and storm or sunshine's ray
　our steps are guided still.

As Abraham and Sarah heard
　the promise of the Lord,
so let our listening hearts be stirred,
still fed by Scripture's every word
　in mind and memory stored.

*As Moses, Aaron, Miriam trod
　a pathway through the sea,
so let us by the light of God
march on to our unseen abode,
　in faith's expectancy.

*Elizabeth's anxiety
　and Zechariah's tongue
were moved to joyful prophecy;
so now with voices glad and free
　our hymns of praise are sung.

As Simeon and Anna came
　to see and share his light,
let us, whose Saviour is the same,
recall his cross and speak his name
　till faith is turned to sight.

As young at heart but full of years
　God's saints have run their race,
like them discarding sins and fears
till Jesus Christ our King appears
　we travel on by grace.

86886 Tune: REPTON

Scriptures: Gen 17:1–8; 18:1–15; 21:1–7   Exod 14:21–22; 15:19–21
Pss 15:1; 84:5–7; 122:1–4   Luke 1:4–25; 57–79; 2:25–38   Heb 12:1–2
Written: Bromley, Aug 2006; revised Feb 2008
First published: *Pilgrim Hymns*, 2007 (original text, but omitting stanzas 3–4)
Yes, 'All-age' (see no.3) must include us seniors! For the origins of this hymn, see nos.24 and
99. It was written and printed as '*Since first we joined in pilgrimage*', and the changes to this
opening stanza and some other lines were the result of scrutiny by TAG. The middle stanzas can he omitted if it proves too long, but the complete text remains my favourite of the
three written for Pilgrim Homes. While concentrating on some of Scripture's influential senior citizens, I hope it is singable by Christians of all ages. With this tune, the last line of each
verse is repeated.

Exodus
Water, fire and blood: the story of our salvation

5 FROM THE WATER COMES THE CHILD

From the water comes the child
born in hope but bound for strife;
God can train the strong, the wild,
leaving death and bringing life.

In the flame the Lord appears,
yet the bush is not consumed:
God is calling, Moses hears;
slaves are loved and tyrants doomed.

When the water turns to blood,
signs of judgement have begun;
when the lamb's blood marks the wood,
safely sleeps the first-born son.

When the flame makes deserts bright
God is here to guard and guide;
cloud by day and fire by night,
see our covenant-God provide!

Through the water we have come;
God has made his people new!
Filled with songs of hope and home,
tell the world what God can do!

7777   Tune: FAIRMILE by David Peacock, or UNIVERSITY COLLEGE

Scriptures: Exod 2–4, 7, 11–15; also Gen 22:14   Ps 96:1–3, 10   Rom 6:2–3
1 Cor 10:1–4
Written: Peckham, Dec 1998
In response to a request from 'Spring Harvest' for hymns on the theme of Exodus. Like most of those written over the years for that annual event, this text did not prove acceptable.

Exodus 3:1–15

Names

6   CROSSING THE DESERT NEAR THE GREAT MOUNTAIN

Crossing the desert
near the great mountain,
I heard a voice speak
out of the flame:
'Moses, I send you
to lead my people!'
'What if they ask me,
What is your name?'

'From everlasting
to everlasting,
I AM your one God,
always the same;
say to my people,
I AM has sent you,
I AM will save you,
that is my name!'

5554D   Tune: BUNESSAN

Scriptures: Exod 3:1–15
Written: Peckham Nov 2000
A song used in primary school assemblies; see no.3 etc. Before enquiring 'Who are you?',
Moses memorably asks 'Who am I?' That would need another song.

Exodus 20:1–17
The Ten Commandments

7 GOD SAYS, 'I SAVED YOU, SET YOU FREE'

God says, 'I saved you, set you free,
and you shall worship none but me.
No image shall you make or serve,
of things around, below, above;
the families who hate me will
continue under judgement still,
but steadfast love shall thousands know
who love me, in my paths to go.'

'You shall not take God's name in vain:
on those who do, guilt must remain.
Remember God's most holy day;
let households learn their Maker's way –
six days for work and one for rest;
the Sabbath and ourselves be blessed.
Honour your parents in the land;
your lives shall prosper at God's hand.'

'You shall not raise your hand to kill
nor plan to do your neighbour ill.
Do not commit adultery;
hold marriage high in purity.
You shall not steal in any form,
nor work with lies your neighbour's harm;
nor make a god of wanton greed
by craving what you do not need.'

'With all your heart love God, your Lord,
his name, his will, his holy word,
your neighbour as yourself, so you
may be a welcome neighbour too.'
Lord, these supreme commands you give
and in their light your children live;
fulfil your law in us, we pray,
with love, by grace, in Christ, today.

LMD   Tune needed

Scriptures: Ex 20:1–17; also Deut 4:5–21; 6:4–5   Mark 12:28–31   Rom 13:8–10   Gal
5:13–14   Col 3:5   Heb 13:1   1 John 3:15
Written: Mainly on trains between Bromley and Cardiff, March 2004.
Becoming aware of a dearth of hymns rooted in the Ten Commandments, and after reading
Brian Edwards' book (1996/2002) *The Ten Commandments for Today*, I attempted to fill
a gap. I hope that the essence of the Decalogue is fairly represented, if not every detail. Another favourite is Thomas Watson's 17th-century *The Ten Commandments* (Banner of Truth
reprint).

Joshua 11:23, 14:15
Rest from war?

8 SO SHALL THE LAND HAVE REST FROM WAR

So shall the land have rest from war,
and truth and peace prevail?
the time is past, when battle-strength
was judged some holy grail.

The time has gone when tribe on tribe
could claim a victor's prize,
with slaughtered flesh on poisoned lands
where every virtue dies.

The aching hearts and longing eyes
of nations everywhere,
of women, men, and boys and girls
want life, not death, to share.

Yet we who cry to God to help
or blame him for our woes
must search elsewhere, recall our votes,
trace where our money goes.

What have we written, said or sung?
What have we failed to do?
Where have we argued, marched, or stood,
or dared to think anew?

The cause of half-demolished homes,
wrecked hospitals, bombed schools,
lies in ourselves; for ruined fields
are made by ruined fools.

So shall the land have rest from war:
some hope – light years away?
Not if, before we cry to God,
we hear God cry today.

CM Tune: LEVAMENTUM, by Sue Gilmurray

Scriptures: Josh 11:23; 14:15 Jas 4:1–3
Written: Paxton (Border) and Bromley, July 2006
First published: *The Anglican Peacemaker* (Anglican Pacifist Fellowship) Oct 2006.
This was suggested by news from Lebanon and Israel while Joshua was part of my daily reading; even in this military book there are hopes of peace. It was begun on holiday and completed at home; Sue Gilmurray soon provided and recorded a tune. It remains more of a song than a hymn. In stanza 7 'ruined' replaces an earlier adjective.

1 Samuel 17:1–50
David and Goliath

9 HAVE YOU HEARD OF A LAD CALLED DAVID?

Have you heard of a lad called David?
He was only a shepherd boy,
but he guarded the sheep very bravely
for he trusted in the Lord most high.
Sing hosanna, sing hosanna,
sing hosanna to the King of kings!
Sing hosanna, sing hosanna,
sing hosanna to the King!

So when David went down to his brothers
he was not very big or tall;
he was tougher than all of the others
for he trusted in the Lord of all.
Sing hosanna...

And when David faced up to the giant
he had only a stone and sling;
though Goliath was huge and defiant,
David trusted in the Lord his King!
Sing hosanna...

Tune: GIVE ME OIL IN MY LAMP / JOY IN MY HEART

Scriptures: 1 Sam 17:1–50
Written: Peckham, SE London, March 2000
For primary school assemblies; one way of presenting this song is for the leader to sing the
verses (and able to give them full expression, varied speed, gestures etc) and the children to
join in the chorus – which completes the theme of Kingship.

1 Kings 1–11
King Solomon

10   HIS NAME IS SOLOMON

His name is Solomon,
King David's son;
no prince so wise as he,
the wealthy one.
And yet for all his gifts
he goes astray;
he will not learn
to walk God's way.
 Solomon, famous one,
 rich in this world's treasure
 but poor to God.

The works of Solomon
are very great;
the temple rises up
in glorious state.
They come to sacrifice,
to praise and pray,
but will not learn
to walk God's way.
 Solomon...

The songs of Solomon
a nation sings;
he writes of cedar trees
and creeping things.
His proverbs speak to us
who live today,
but will we learn
to walk God's way?
 Solomon...

The Son of Solomon,
the Son of God,
more wise, more glorious,
the eternal Word;
the temple he creates
will not decay;
he is our song,
he is God's way.
 Jesus Christ, Lord of all,
 live in us, we pray, that
 we walk with God.

Tune: CEDARS by Anne Greenidge (2005),
or SOLOMON by Christopher Hayward (2005)

Scriptures: 2 Sam 12:24   selected vv in 1 Kgs and 2 Chr   1 Chr 29:21–25
Pss 72, 127   Prov 1:1–7   Song 1:1   Matt 1:1–6; 12:42   Mark 1:1
John 1:1–2; 2:18–22
Written: Bromley, March 2005
When Chris Hayward asked for a new hymn about King Solomon for use at Christ Church
Blackburn, I turned first to a tune composed by Anne Greenidge for a school hymn – see
nos.65 and 98. This dictated its distinctive metre; Chris then wrote his own tune at Black-
burn where the words were first used.

1 Kings 3:4–15
More than he asked or thought

11   WHEN SOLOMON CAME TO BE KING OF ALL ISRAEL

When Solomon came to be king of all Israel
the Lord showed him mercy and searched out his mind:
'Whatever you want, you must ask me to give you' –
a foretaste of what every Christian can find.

He asked not for riches, for long life or glory,
but only for wisdom in ruling the land;
to be the Lord's servant, to know good from evil,
the mind of a monarch who could understand.

So God gave King Solomon wisdom to govern,
a heart of discernment, the answer to prayer;
and what he did not ask, that too God provided,
both riches and honour most glorious and rare.

God grant we may long for the things that are needful,
your will and your kingdom, and praying, believe
your energy gives us far more in Christ Jesus
than words can convey or our minds can conceive.

12 11 12 11   Tune: STREETS OF LAREDO, or a new tune?

Scriptures: 1 Kgs 3:4–15 and 2 Chr 1:1–12; also John 14:13–14; 15:16; 16:23–24
Eph 3:20
Written: Stanzas 2–4, March 2005; revised May 2005 with new 1st stanza; again in Nov 2005.
See the notes to no.10. This one began with stanza 2, but TAG preferred a clearer opening which named Solomon from the start. Hence came a new beginning and other revisions.

Nehemiah 8
This is the word of the Lord

12 IN THE PUBLIC SQUARE THEY MEET

In the public square they meet:
let us join them, listen, look –
Ezra rises to his feet,
opening up the mighty book;
    All are standing, hands are raised,
    'God, our mighty Lord, be praised!'

Scribe and Levites read and teach
covenant-promise, law and psalm;
to the hearts the Scriptures reach,
God makes bare his holy arm:
    'Do not mourn or weep' they say;
    'God has met with us this day!'

'Praise our God, Amen!' they sing;
'Amen!' echoes round the wall:
then they bow down, worshipping,
wonder in the minds of all.
    Through the morning hours they hear
    every word of God made clear.

So a ransomed nation hears,
understands and celebrates;
spreads the news and dries its tears,
far beyond the city gates:
    through the land, its breadth and length,
    joy from God is all their strength.

Captives once, like them set free,
up to Zion we have come;
Christ has won our liberty,
covenant grace has brought us home:
    like them, let us hear God's voice;
    trust, repent, obey, rejoice!

88 88 88 Tune: DIX

Scriptures: Neh 8; also Ezra 7:6–10   Isa 51:11; 52:9–10   Heb 4:12; 12:22–25
Written: Peckham, Mar 2001
Lance Pierson at Christ Church Old Kent Rd (1998) and Neil Richards at East St Baptist
Church, Walworth (2001), were visiting speakers who differently but vividly brought Nehemiah ch.8 memorably to life. After many revisions with the Bible open in front of me I
settled on this text in March 2001, and first sang it in July at Crockenhill Baptist Church
when I was the visitor, courtesy of Malcolm Jones. As well as echoes of Isaiah, the final lines
use Hebrews 12 to strike a contemporary note; we can enter the story today.

Psalm 1
Two ways to live (2; see no.1)

13 BLESSED, EACH ONE WHO DOES NOT WALK

Blessed, each one who does not walk
where the ungodly hold their talk,
stand in wait where sinners meet,
sit where cynics take their seat;
Lord, your law their joy they find,
day and night it shapes their mind.

Come, each true believer see
as a firmly-planted tree;
flowing waters, crystal clear,
make it fruitful year by year:
green, unfading, are its leaves;
boundless grace all good achieves.

Evildoers are not so;
chaff that flies when breezes blow
in God's judgement cannot thrive,
with his flock will not survive:
God knows all his children's path;
paths of evil end in wrath.

77 77 77 Tune: ENGLAND'S LANE

Scriptures: Psalm 1; also Josh 1:8   Ps 119:16,35   Jer 17:5–8
Written: Peckham, 1 Nov (All Saints) 1999
Requested by Christopher Hayward for use the following day at Oak Hill Theological College, where Dick Lucas was due to preach on this Psalm; apparently no existing and available version would do. So I wrote it that morning. Among key decisions: the 3-stanza structure; choice of the first word; omitting 'righteous' and 'wicked' for different reasons; and using singular but inclusive language. Most other versions are either masculine or plural.

Psalm 19:7–11

A song about treasure

14 DEARER THAN GOLD ARE THE WORDS OF THE LORD

Dearer than gold are the words of the Lord,	Ps 19:7–11
sweeter than honey to me	
treasure and wisdom and wealth and reward;	
they give me light – I can see!	Ps 119:105

Hallelujah, Hallelujah ...   (etc: repeat chorus after 1st and last verses only?)

Treasure from God is the kingdom of heaven,	Matt 13:44
hidden from sight in the earth;	
when we have found how our sins are forgiven,	
nothing can equal its worth.	

Don't store up treasure for life on this earth,	Matt 6:19–21
ready for thieves, moth and rust.	
Riches in heaven are of far greater worth;	
Christ is the treasure to trust.	

Look to the prize and not back to the past;	1 Cor 9:24–25; Phil 3:12–14
God has our treasure in store:	1 Pet 1:4
go for the crown of the life that will last,	Jas 1:12
trust in his love more and more.	

Hallelujah, Hallelujah ...

Tune: SEEK YE FIRST THE KINGDOM OF GOD

Scriptures: see marginal notes
Written: Peckham, March 2001
This was a response to a request from Deborah Woolley of East Street Baptist Church in Walworth (see also nos.90 and 91), who was on the look out for more children's songs on the theme of 'Treasure', to use in Holiday Bible Clubs, etc. It can be taken one verse at a time.

Psalm 62
Security in God

15 FIND REST, MY SOUL, IN GOD ALONE

Find rest, my soul, in God alone,
my hope and my salvation;
my refuge, strength and health is he,
so how can I be shaken?

How long will thieves attack a man
and claim him as their victim?
With poisoned heart and mind and mouth
they plot to undermine him.

Both slaves and sovereigns are mere wind,
celebrities, all empty.
Don't trust in vast or tainted wealth;
God is our gold, our plenty.

And all my good depends on him,
my God, my goal, my giver;
my castle, cave and towering cliff –
so trust in him for ever!

Two things I hear and I believe,
that God is strong, and loving.
In him we find our true reward
and his great day is coming.

In truth, my soul waits still on God;
from God comes my salvation.
My refuge, strength and health is he
and I shall not be shaken.

8787 iambic   Tune: ST COLUMBA, or new tune?

Scriptures: Psalm 62; also Ps 37:7   Eccles 2:17–26   Isa 2:12; 12:2   Matt 11:28
Written: Bromley, Aug 2005; revised Nov 2005
A text arising from my daily reading in 2004, when I jotted down some draft lines beginning 'In truth, my soul waits still on God', it was rearranged to its present form with help
from TAG.

Psalm 90:12

Numbering and naming our days

16 AS SPECIAL DAYS ADORN THE YEAR

As special days adorn the year
we mark their passing by our prayer:
each sunset, our homecoming sign;
each dawn, a story's opening line.

All doors invite us in to pray;
each path is marked the pilgrims' way:
we walk with patience, and await
the upward arrow on each gate.

Each week brings anniversaries
of harvest, unity or peace;
we worship while it is today,
for tides and times do not delay.

If Thursday may remind us still
of upper room, or tree or hill;
then Friday moves our hearts to weep
but Sunday rouses us from sleep:

This weekly Easter, day of light,
scatters the darkness of the night;
the Hallelujah chorus rings
the globe, while all Christ's body sings.

So now all years are years of grace
and every room a sacred space.
Where God is, holy ground is here;
let Christ be welcomed everywhere!

LM   Tune: WAREHAM, or new tune?

Scriptures: Ps 90:12   2 Cor 6:1–2

Written: Bromley, Oct 2005

'Every place is hallowed ground' we sing with William Cowper. Ironically, though, many pilgrims tread the special places he loved (home, study, garden, parish church) where a special atmosphere seems to prevail as his gentle, vulnerable influence lingers on within and around Olney's remarkable 'Newton and Cowper Museum'.
Even 1779, the year of those Olney Hymns, is well remembered and commemorated. My text is an attempt to
express some of the ambivalence of these special times and locations in a world and life-span which all belongs
to God. And those ritual-free New Testament believers met on the first day of the week.

Psalm 102
I am in distress; God is in control

17 LORD, HEAR MY PRAYER! MY CRY SHALL COME BEFORE YOU

LORD, hear my prayer! My cry shall come before you;
hide not your face when I am in distress.
My life burns up; my days have lost their glory,
drifting like smoke, in pain and helplessness.

Like some wild owl among deserted ruins,
lonely I call while enemies curse on.
Tears are my drink; God's wrath is my undoing;
ashes my food till all my days are gone.

But you, O Lord, remain enthroned for ever;
you will arise; in you shall kingdoms trust.
Now is the time; your city pleads your favour;
your servants love her stones, her very dust.

God will rebuild! Write this to sing tomorrow;
lips yet unformed their Hallelujahs cry!
Glory will dawn upon our world of sorrow,
freeing from prison those condemned to die.

Then shall your name on Zion's hill be spoken;
strangers shall fill Jerusalem with praise.
But as for me, my strength is bruised and broken;
spare me, O God; do not cut short my days.

Heaven and earth you formed in the beginning;
these soon wear out – Lord, you remain the same!
They shall be changed; your years endure unending;
our children's children live to praise your name.

11 10 11 10 Tune: STRENGTH AND STAY, or INTERCESSOR

Scriptures: Psalm 102; also Ps 56:8   Luke 2:26   Heb 1:10–12; 13:8
Written: Peckham, June–July 1998
First published: *Praise!*, 2000.
This was a late submission for *Praise!*, a hymn-book which includes a version of all 150 Psalms, whole or in part.
I was asked to attempt a new approach to one which had not proved easy or popular to paraphrase. Like the
130th, this 102nd begins in the depths but concludes in confidence – with good reason. Its glory is found in its
New Testament application in Hebrews 1. The opening lines were my starting point which suggested the rhythm
and metre; among those providing helpful input were Brian Edwards, David Preston, Jim Sayers and (as ever)
Marjorie. Are we over-fond of our visible 'churches', their 'very dust'? The magazine *Barnabas Aid* noted in 2006
that 'Christians in situations of persecution rarely if ever argue against the value of church buildings'.

Psalm 109
My accusers; my God

18 HOW WICKEDLY THEY SPREAD THEIR LIES

How wickedly they spread their lies
and speak with vicious tongue!
My prayer, my friendship they despise
and do me groundless wrong.
  I praise my God, but I implore:
  do not stay silent any more.

How terribly will they be shamed
when they are justly tried!
Their days are shortened, prayers
                    condemned,
the accuser at their side.
  The traitor dies in deep disgrace,
  so let another take his place.

How fearfully we hear the doom
on all their kith and kin!
Their work, their wealth, their name,
                    their home
all suffer for their sin.
  They did not bless – and reaped the
  blame;
    they loved to curse – and curses came.

How tenderly the LORD will deal
with us, when stalked by death!
The wounded he will lift and heal,
the fainting, fill with breath.
  I plead your love, your name alone:
  save me, my God! Your power make
                    known!

How graciously your hand will bless
when my accusers curse!
Dishonour is their chosen dress;
their slanders you reverse.
  I praise the LORD who judges them;
  when God defends, who shall condemn?

86 86 88 Tune: TYDI A RODDAIST, or PEMBROKE

Scriptures: Ps 109; also Luke 10:33–34   Acts 1:15–26   Rom 8:33–34   Rev 12:10
Written: Peckham, June 1998
First published: *Praise!* 2000
'This Psalm spares us nothing' – Derek Kidner. Partly for this reason, it proved one of the
hardest, and the last, for which to find an acceptable version for *Praise!*. As in many older
paraphrases, the imprecations in the Scripture text are treated here as statements of fact and
solemn warning. This was the first item I had written for 6 months, and the first since *Light
upon the River* went to press.

Psalm 111
God sent redemption

19 WITH ALL MY HEART I PRAISE THE LORD

With all my heart I praise the LORD,
here with the saints, his deeds proclaim;
great are his works, and great his word:
    those who treasure them, they will ponder them: Hallelujah!

Glorious is God! We shout his name,
his everlasting righteousness;
changeless in grace, in truth the same;
    O remember his saving miracles: Hallelujah!

All those who fear him, God will bless,
raise us to glory from the dust,
feed us and grant us true success;
    he remembers his holy covenant: Hallelujah!

All that God does is true and just;
laws that will stand eternally,
all that God speaks our hearts can trust,
    we his people and he our Rescuer: Hallelujah!

God sent redemption, true and free,
covenant grace endures always:
holy his name, our God is he;
    crucial Sacrifice, mighty Exodus: Hallelujah!

Let the LORD's precepts rule our days –
wisdom begins by fearing God;
God shall have everlasting praise:
    Hallelujah, Hallelujah, Hallelujah!

888 with Hallelujahs   Tune: VULPIUS

Scriptures: Ps 111; also Exod 2:24   Dan 9:24   Job 28:28   Prov 9:10   Luke 1:68; 9:31
Written: Peckham, Feb 2001
Like Psalm 96, the 111th is one where thoughts come in threes; always a problem for the foursquare metrical paraphrases. I wrote a version of this in 1982 (eightsquare!), 'Hallelujah, praise the Lord.' Then I was struck afresh by the Psalm in my daily reading, and settled on the tune as being a joyful 3-liner, plus of course Hallelujahs. The original Hebrew is acrostic or alphabetical; the rhyme scheme here is not instantly obvious. Trying it out at Blackburn 4 years later, one participant said that we could hardly expect to attract a new generation if we persisted with tunes like this. Friends, I love it; but the floor is yours.

Psalm 117
Acrostic praise

20   O PRAISE THE LORD; PROCLAIMED, ADORED

> O praise the LORD;
>
> Proclaimed, adored,
>
> Redeemer God!
>
> All lands, sing loud
>
> Immanuel's name,
>
> Spread far his fame.
>
> Earth's people, sing
>
> To heaven's King;
>
> His faithfulness
>
> Each tongue confess,
>
> Love, mercy, grace,
>
> Our hearts embrace;
>
> Rejoice always,
>
> Declare God's praise!

44 in couplets   Tune: CROFTON LANE, by Linda Mawson

Scriptures: Ps 117; also Ps 19:4   Dan 4:37   Matt 1:23   Phil 4:4   1 Thess 5:16
Written: Peckham, Dec 2000
Almost exactly 400 years ago Mary Herbert, Countess of Pembroke, wrote some outstanding Psalm paraphrases, completing a volume started by her brother Sir Philip Sidney who had reached Ps 42 when he died in 1586. They remained almost unknown until the 1960s, but included an almost playful acrostic of 'Prais' the Lord' for Ps 117. After failing to find a way to modernise her version, I tried to produce a new one of my own.

Psalm 135

The one true God

21 SING ONCE AGAIN, GOD'S NAME BE PRAISED

Sing once again, God's name be praised,
all who serve the living Lord;
Hallelujah! sing the glory
of the One supremely good;
Hallelujah, sing again!
   Jacob's people, treasured prize,
   chosen as God's very own
   by the One uniquely great,
   Light eternal, God alone:
Hallelujah, sing again!

Low on the earth and high in heaven,
restless ocean, pathless plain,
God does always what he pleases,
sends the lightning, storm and rain;
Hallelujah, sing again!
   Egypt's firstborn met their doom,
   Pharaoh saw God's outstretched hand;
   famous kings and nations died,
   Israel gained their promised land;
Hallelujah, sing again!

Your name O Lord, for ever stands,
families pass on your fame;
God will vindicate his servants,
hope of all who trust that name.
Hallelujah, sing again!
   Shrines of silver, gods of gold,
   dumb their mouths and deaf their ears,
   shaped by mortal mind and hand,
   blind their eyes, no breath is theirs;
so are all who trust in them.

Israel of God, come, bless the Lord!
Royal priesthood, praise your King,
Father, Son and Holy Spirit:
fear and worship, shout and sing
Hallelujah, sing again!
   Heirs of new Jerusalem,
   look to Christ on Zion's hill;
   all who serve that sacred house
   with the angels, praise him still;
Hallelujah, sing Amen!

87877 77777 Tune: FLOREAS FETTESIA,
by Arthur H Mann (1850–1929).

Scripture: Ps 135; also Exod 19:3–6   Pss 115:3–8; 136
Heb 12:1–2; 22–24   1 Pet 2:9–10
Written: Bromley, May 2007
Fettes College, Edinburgh, has some distinguished former pupils, among them Michael Lumgair who in 2006 retired to Bromley from his parish of St Peter Bexleyheath. He asked if I could set the fine tune of the school song to some new words for Christian congregations to sing; the original Latin by E W Howson was first sung in 1881. A Psalm seemed to be called for; the 135th commended itself partly by its medium length. Assisted by a fine CD recording I set to work, viewing the Psalm from a New Testament perspective, and the text was launched at Christ Church Beckenham, where the Lumgairs then belonged, in Sept 2007.

Ecclesiastes 4:9–12

God's arithmetic

22 HERE I AM, ALL ALONE

Here I am, all alone,
can't do this job on my own;
but if you come with me, it'll soon be
    done –
two can do much more than one!

Here we are, just us two;
there is still so much to do,
but if you can join us, then there will be
    three:
we can do it – just you see!

One plus two, making three,
work together happily,
but for some things we need just a little
    more;
can you come and make it four?

Can you see four of us
get things done without a fuss?
But we sometimes meet things bigger
    than they seem;
five of us will make a team!

Watch us work, famous five,
we're the finest five alive,
till we find some things we're never
    going to lift;
two more hands will make them shift!

Counting up, now we're six,
see what we can fetch and fix,
but there's always room for many, many
    more –
seven, eight, nine, ten, or a score!

Jesus called twelve to start,
hundreds, thousands, play a part –
if the work is worth it, getting anywhere,
everyone can take a share!

Tune: THIS OLD MAN, HE PLAYED ONE
(KNICK KNACK, PADDY WHACK, GIVE A DOG A BONE)

Scriptures: Eccles 4:9–12   Mark 3:13–19   Gal 6:2   Phil 4:3
Written: Peckham, 1999
First published: *Hunger for Justice*, 2004.
Head Teacher Pauline Doidge of Pilgrims' Way Primary School in the Old Kent Road (where
our first two sons started nearly 30 years before) wanted a new song about how we need
one another. So this is a progressive/cumulative/action text where a solitary leader begins
sadly, then calls a child out during verse 1, another in verse 2 etc, then a group in verse 6
until it all ends in happy confusion. The children must be warned that they have to be quick!
This may lack Biblical meat – but it proved useful at some special public events, and we can
emphasise the crucial 'Jesus' in the last verse.

Isaiah 1–12

The King is coming

23 HEAR, YOU HEAVENS, AND LISTEN, EARTH

'Hear, you heavens, and listen, earth!'
  When will people understand?
  here is truth for every land:
we have turned our backs on God;
  nations, sick from head to toe,
  filled with sores and wounds and woe.

Rituals, rules and slogans fail;
  'Let us reason' says the Lord;
  'Wash you clean; obey my word':
From his mountain God will judge,
  teach his ways, his paths of peace,
  weapons, wars, and strife will cease.

For the day of God will dawn,
  sovereign justice reach to all,
  wealth will rot and pride will fall,
mortals hide and idols fail;
  let this world do what it can;
  God is here – and what is man?

Who is this, the virgin's Son?
  Root and Branch and fruitful Vine,
  God's anointed, heaven's Sign:
Light in darkness, Prince of peace,
  born for us, and Spirit-filled,
  God with us, a little child!

'Holy, holy, holy Lord!'
  All that I have heard and seen
  finds me guilty, lost, unclean.
Now you heal my lips with fire,
  bear my sins, become my friend;
  I will go where you will send.

I will praise and give you thanks,
  God my joy who makes me strong,
  God my Saviour and my song.
Show the nations who he is,
  all he says and all he's done:
  God with us, the holy One!

777 777   Tune: BLACKBURN, by Christopher Hayward

Scriptures: Isa 1–12
Written: Bromley, Aug 2004
One of Chris Hayward's urgent requests came from Blackburn, Lancs, in 2004 – a hymn covering the main themes of the first 12 chapters of Isaiah? I had already touched on chs.1, 6 and 12; 9 seemed well-provided for. This response was promptly set to music by Chris and used at Christ Church, Blackburn. The singular pronouns in stanzas 5–6 accord with the prophet's own emphasis, but the whole text may remain for somewhat specialist use.

Isaiah 46:4
Sustained into old age

24   LORD JESUS CHRIST, IF DAY OR NIGHT

Lord Jesus Christ, if day or night
bring anxious thoughts to mind,
grant us to trust you, and delight
in new joys yet to find.
    And help us, Lord, if looking back
    we feel a sense of loss;
    enriched by you, we have no lack –
    there stands your empty cross.

Help, Lord, if we are slow to give
the thanks which are your due;
the blessings every hour we live
are loving gifts from you.
    And help when smaller things go wrong,
    if we are quick to blame,
    to know forgiveness swift and strong
    and mercy in your name.

Help, Lord, and give us eyes to see
that we are not alone;
since you are ours, so shall we be
content to be your own.
    Lord Jesus Christ, if we forget
    the gospel of your grace,
    remind, renew, prepare us yet
    to greet you face to face.

CMD   Tune: KINGSFOLD

Scriptures: Pss 22:2; 130:4 Isa 46:4   Matt 28:20   Acts 20:24   1 Cor 13:12   Jas 1:17
Written: Bromley, June–Aug 2006, revised March 2008
Offered in response to a request for new hymns for the 200th anniversary in 2007 of the Pilgrim Homes for elderly Christians; see also nos.4 and 99. The revision owes much to TAG.

Jeremiah 29:7 (1)

The welfare of the city

25 IS THE CITY ALL THEY SAY IT IS – JUST DIRT AND NOISE?

Is the city all they say it is – just dirt and noise?
Is there hope for all its men and women, girls and boys?
    Do our neighbours live in fear
    of new dangers lurking near?
Is there beauty in the city such as God enjoys?

Can our streets and parks be safe, our schools and churches strong?
And wherever we are from, can everyone belong?
    Does the city need a soul?
    Can what's broken be made whole?
Will it stagger down to hell, or dance to heaven's song?

Didn't Jesus love the city, in those three short years
when it half-believed his stories, when it felt his tears?
    But it couldn't take the heat
    and it nailed his hands and feet;
then on Sunday – Hallelujah! – that's his voice it hears!

So today those hands bring us together, team by team,
and those feet we aim to follow, fleshing out God's dream.
    By the Holy Spirit's flame
    go to work in Jesus' name
for a city where the Lord of love will rule supreme.

Tune: KELVINGROVE

Scriptures: Pss 22:16; 55:9–11   Jer 29:7   Ezek 48:35   Zech 8:1–5
Matt 23:37   Luke 19:41–42; 24:39   Rom 12:4–5   1 Pet 2:21
Written: Bromley, Aug 2004
The 2004 'Soul in the City' brought thousands of young people to London from many nations, for two summer weeks of mission and service. They reached as far as Bromley, one of
the outer-London boroughs, and when I joined the washers-up at the school where our local
team was based, leader Simon Jones said 'We could do with a hymn for this'. By mid-week
I found he was serious, even suggesting the tune. Next Sunday my effort was sung at Bromley Baptist Church where Simon was Senior Pastor. One local reference (to Princes Plain) was
later ironed out to make the text more widely usable.

Jeremiah 29:7 (2)
Urban beauty

26   IN THE HEARTBEAT OF THE CITY

In the heartbeat of the city
through its rhythm and its beauty,
for the lowly and the mighty
    comes the gracious peace of God.

To its life of noise and clamour,
in the style or in the squalor,
from the Lord of grace and valour
    comes the gentle peace of God.

In our music and our trouble
through the restless hours of travel,
to the busy and the brittle
    comes the healing peace of God.

Through the streets that make us weary,
in the burdens we must carry,
by the cross of Christ our glory
    comes the lasting peace of God.

In the welcome and the washing,
at the bread and wine for sharing,
by the word of God for hearing
    comes the perfect peace of God.

8887 Tune: OLD YEAVERING, by Noël Tredinnick

Scriptures: Isa 26:3   Jer 29:7   John 14:27   Gal 6:1–5, 14
Written: Limehouse, 1988
I am always sad when the city is associated only with ugliness – see the previous item – or when peace is thought to be reside where people are few or absent! So this is an urban response to, or counterpart of, Michael Perry's 'Like a mighty river flowing'; though written more than twenty years ago, it has not seen the light of day until now. Line 1 is revised from 'Through the throbbing of the city'.

Daniel 1–6, 12

Serving and speaking for God in dangerous times

27 IN EXILE FROM THEIR HOMES

In exile from their homes,
exposed to pagan eyes,
God's servants wait; his favour comes
with health to make them wise.
On trial through dangerous days
they fear no dreams of kings;
their work is prayer, their joy is praise,
from God their courage springs.

Where idols are built up
and blasphemy is law,
they face the flames, affirm their hope,
and fill their foes with awe.
When walking with the great
their witness does not fail;
to powers that be, they demonstrate
God's kingdom must prevail.

Where judgements stir the land
and trembling shakes the throne,
the Most High holds us in his hand
and makes his purpose known.
When prayer is disallowed,
let powers do what they please;
we need not ape the faithless crowd
but fall upon our knees.

So Daniel and the three
endured as they began;
their God is ours! By faith we see
and serve the Son of Man,
till all the wise shall shine
like stars for evermore;
with those who point the way divine,
one Saviour we adore.

SMD Tune: DARETOBE by Christopher Hayward

Scriptures: Dan 1–6; also Dan 7:13–14; 12:3
Written: Peckham, Jan 2001
Except for 'The glorious God of heaven' (*Light upon the River* no.55, written in 1974) this
was the first of my 'Daniel' texts to be written, responding to Chris Hayward's urgent (as
usual) request for a hymn on this book. A sermon series was due at St James's Muswell Hill,
N London; this text gives 4 lines, or half a stanza, to each of the first 6 chapters, concluding with 8 lines on chs.7 and 12. With Chris's new tune it was duly sung on 11 Feb, and later
at the annual 'Word Alive' gathering in 2005, when Jonathan Fletcher expounded the Book
of Daniel.

Daniel 7
Son of Man, Ancient of Days

28 WHAT DANIEL HAS SEEN IN VISIONS BY NIGHT

What Daniel has seen in visions by night,
whatever they mean, their truth he must write:
four beasts from the ocean devour all they find;
their cruel commotion still troubles our mind.

But see! One they name the Ancient of Days,
whose throne is all flame, his pathway ablaze:
great throngs in procession, the Judge at their head;
his court is in session, the books will be read.

The beasts and the kings have met their last hour,
their teeth and their wings are shorn of their power.
And look! – in the vision, the true Son of Man,
completing his mission, perfecting God's plan.

He comes on the cloud, approaching the throne,
still bruised but unbowed, no longer unknown.
His is the dominion, whom nations obey;
his glorious kingdom shall not pass away.

The end is not yet; the earth still has strife,
new beasts roar their threats to tear out our life.
But saints throughout history who serve the Most High
shall fathom the mystery, shall live and not die.

10 10 11 10   Tune: HANOVER

Scriptures: Dan 7; also Mark 13:24–27; 14:61–62   Heb 12:28   Rev 1:5–7
Written: Oxford and Peckham, Aug–Sept 2001
For the background, see notes to no.27. This was the first of the series to be written, and
the first to be sung at Muswell Hill.

Daniel 7–12
Prophecy

29 AT MANY TIMES, IN VARIOUS WAYS

At many times, in various ways,
God spoke to us in former days;
by dream and vision, sound and sight
which spelled disaster or delight.
    So if the message carries weight
    its spokesman must be advocate;
    small wonder if the prophet's fears
    spill out in trembling and in tears.

But faithfully he draws the scene
in words, half-knowing what they mean;
God's Spirit moves the heart to seek,
the ears to hear, the voice to speak
    of figures human and divine
    revealed in symbol, shape and sign,
    and wonders hard to comprehend
    of earth's beginning and its end.

And as we scan each living page
let thoughts and prayers and praise engage
with warnings as with promises,
for one great light outshines all these:
    though lions, kings and armies roar,
    God rules, and loves for evermore;
    let him be ours, and we his own,
    all lands acclaim him Lord alone!

LMD   Tune needed

Scriptures: Daniel 7–12; also Ps 99:1 Heb 1:1 2 Pet 1:19–20
Written: Peckham, Sept 2001
Originally in 4 stanzas of LM, this further response to Chris Hayward's request (see no.27) was thoroughly revised in Sept 2004 after comments from TAG.

Daniel 8
Strange sights: true insights

30 THE LORD ONCE GAVE THE VISION

The Lord once gave the vision –
a river, goat and ram,
two horns in fierce collision
and worship made a sham:
but holy ones, with Gabriel,
a Prince, a glorious land;
among us, who is able
or wise to understand?

Earth's tyrannies are grievous
but times draw near their end;
dictators and deceivers
their empires still extend:
the watchmen long have slumbered,
the lamp of God burns dim;
but days of wrong are numbered,
the last word rests with him.

How can we face the future
in such a world as this
when, worse than brutes, we butcher,
while good things go amiss?
But Daniel knew he never
need fear an earthly thing;
let us put first, for ever,
the business of our King.

76 76 D   Tune: CRÜGER

Scriptures: Dan 8; also 1 Sam 3:3   Matt 6:33   Luke 21:9–11
Written: Oxford and Peckham, Aug–Sept 2001
Being quite narrowly focused, this next part of the 'Daniel' series (nos.27 onwards) may
never be a top favourite. But I wrote it to complete the challenge of this remarkable book,
and in order not to evade the issues raised by this chapter.

Daniel 9
Confession for a nation

31 DANIEL THE PROPHET BOWED IN PRAYER

Daniel the prophet bowed in prayer
to confess a nation's sin;
but when we dare approach your throne,
Lord, where shall we begin?
    Hear, O Lord; O Lord, forgive!
    Our God, do not delay!
    For your name's sake, by whom we live,
    have mercy, Lord, today!

Israel ignored what Scripture said
and rebelled against your laws:
theirs was the guilt, the shame, the dread;
the mercy, Lord, was yours.
    Hear, O Lord; O Lord, forgive!
    Our God, do not delay!
    Your promised covenant revive;
    have mercy, Lord, today!

As in the exile years, so now
we have come before your throne;
to seek your face we humbly bow
and plead your grace alone.
    Hear, O Lord, O Lord, forgive!
    In Jesus' name we pray:
    for us he died, in him we live;
    have mercy, Lord, today!

Tune: MARY'S BOY CHILD

Scriptures: Daniel 9; also Ezra 9   Neh 9   2 Cor 5:15   Heb 4:14–16
Written: Aug–Sept 2001
One of a group written at Chris Hayward's request; this one for the church of St James
Muswell Hill, N London. The choice of tune was mine.

Daniel 10

By the great river

32 WHEN WE ENCOUNTER THE WONDER OF PROPHECY

When we encounter the wonder of prophecy
truth from the Lord may be hard to endure:
Daniel was mourning and fasting in penitence;
clear was the vision, the message most sure.

By the great river, and marked on the calendar,
known on the map, this formidable sight:
here stands a stranger in glorious radiance,
voice like a multitude, face of pure light.

Touched by his hand is the prophet of Israel;
summoned by name, he is shaken and stirred:
'Man dearly loved, do not fear! I am sent to you;
since you have trembled, your prayer has been heard.'

Speechless and strengthless, God's servant is listening;
his lips are touched, like Isaiah's, to speak.
He must stand upright, be strong and obedient,
with the invincible power of the meek.

O God, forgive, when we rush into ministry
with no repentance, no trembling, no shame;
teach us to listen, to pray and wait silently –
then boldly witness to your saving name.

12 10 12 10   Tune: WAS LEBET

Scriptures: Dan 10; also Isa 6:1–8   Jer 23:22   Ezek 1:1; 2:1–5   2 Cor 4:1   Rev 1:12–19
Written: Peckham, Aug–Sept 2001
See notes for the 'Daniel' sequence at no.27.

Daniel 11
Judge of the nations

33 NEWS FROM THE SOUTH AND THE NORTH

News from the south and the north,
wars in the east and the west –
what will the morning bring forth?
Still must God's poor be oppressed?

God calls the nations his own,
God made the land and the sea;
God rules the skies, and his throne
stands, and for ever shall be.

God is the Judge of us all;
we only live by his breath:
tyrants must come at his call,
flatterers fail at their death.

Which of these lords recognised
God the once-visible Word?
Praise be to God and his Christ!
Praise where the Gospel is heard!

Still must believers endure
prison and burning and sword;
still their refining is sure,
finding their joy in their Lord.

Knowing their God, they are strong;
knowing their God, they resist:
though pain and peril seem long,
idols shall cease to exist.

Are north and south still at war,
east and west locked into strife?
Judge us and save us once more,
Christ our Good News, and our Life!

7777 dactyl   Tune needed

Scriptures: Dan 11; also Ps 95:3–4   Mark 13:7–8   Acts 4:24–30; 17:24–31
Heb 11:36–40   1 Pet 1:6–9
Written: Peckham, Aug–Sept 2001
See the note to no.27. It was not easy to include the themes of Daniel 11 in a general hymn
about the prophet; wars between north and south, interpreted more globally, have a grimly
contemporary ring.

Daniel 12
Then comes the end

34 SOON COMES THE TIME OF THE ARCHANGEL MICHAEL

Soon comes the time of the archangel Michael,
prince and protector through stormcloud and strife;
great the distress but far greater the mercy
promised to all found in God's book of life.

All who have slept in the dust shall be woken,
some to disgrace, some to laughter and light;
those who are wise will be shining in glory,
those who win souls, like the stars in the night.

Till then the world will be seething in turmoil,
knowledge expanding, but wisdom most rare;
seasons and years which are known to the Father,
mysteries unfolding for all in his care.

Then comes the end, the last prayer, the last preaching,
sealed in his book till the last of the days;
thanks be to God for each page from his prophets,
praise for his words, for his wonders be praise!

What is our part in this drama of heaven,
warnings of judgement and windows of grace?
Watching and witnessing, suffering and loving,
serving our King till we meet face to face.

11 10 11 10 Tune: O QUANTA QUALIA

Scriptures: Dan 12; also Mark 13:7–10 Luke 10:20 John 5:28–29
Phil 4:3 Rev 5:1–5; 12:7–9
Written: Peckham, Aug 2001; revised Bromley Aug 2004
'Multitudes who sleep in the dust of the earth will awake...Those who are wise will shine like the brightness of the heavens...'; these and other stirring, searching prophecies from the final chapter of Daniel moved me to complete the series begun in 2001 in response to Chris Hayward's request; see no.27 etc. This text was revised in Aug 2004 in response to comments from TAG; because of the domino effect of adjusting a single line, only seven of the original 20 remained entirely unchanged.

Joel (1)
A prophet for harvest and Pentecost (1)

35   DAY OF THE LORD, HOW SHALL WE KNOW YOUR COMING

Day of the Lord, how shall we know your coming,
how shall we see your final dawn appear?
Angry with fire and heaven's thunder drumming,
dark with the doom of judgement drawing near?

So once the prophet Joel saw in vision
locust and famine sweeping through the land,
multitudes, gathered for a last decision,
saw and proclaimed the Lord's great day at hand.

Then with an eye beyond disaster ranging,
faith saw the Spirit on all flesh outpoured;
viewed all the land from dearth to beauty changing,
under the loving impulse of the Lord.

Old men dream dreams from heaven's inspiration,
young men see visions of God's reign to be,
maidens enjoy the wonders of salvation,
servants, the Spirit's breath of liberty.

Day of the Spirit, we have seen your glory,
stirring from hearts ablaze with holy flame,
kindling the lips that tell the gospel story,
glowing in lives which bear the Saviour's name.

Still we await the day of consummation,
one mighty act of judgement on the earth;
when God brings in the longed-for new creation
to make an end, and glorious rebirth.

Christ will be judge; his work by death completed
shall in that day alone avail for plea.
While there is time, ask now how we have treated
him who endured the night of Calvary.

11 10 11 10   Tune: LORD OF THE YEARS, or new tune?

Scriptures: Joel; also Jer 31:12–13   John 5:22   Acts 2:14–21   Rev 21:1
Written: Peckham Oct 2000; revised Bromley April 2008
St James' Church Muswell Hill, N London, studied the book of Joel in autumn 2000. The by-then-usual-and-urgent phone call from Chris Hayward required a new hymn or song; preceded by Albert Bayly and now succeeded by Timothy Dudley-Smith, this was one of the two I offered. It remained dormant, however until I revised it (mainly stanza 6) in preparation for the present book; see the following item.

Joel (2)
A prophet for harvest and Pentecost (2)

36 THE PROPHET SPEAKS; THE LOCUSTS COME

The prophet speaks, the locusts come;
the fields are bare, the farmers numb,
the olives fail, the ground is dry,
the vineyards rot, the orchards die,
the people grieve, their leaders cry.
For the Lord has spoken;
the day is near
and the day will come,
for the Lord is here!

The trumpets sound their clear alarm:
the day of gloom, the coming storm.
'But even now', the Lord declares,
'Return to me with heartfelt tears:
I will restore your wasted years!'
For the Lord...

The Lord is good, his love is pure,
his anger slow, his mercy sure;
Be glad in him who gives the rain
as seasons yield their fruits again,
and harvests, gold with ripening grain.
For the Lord...

And afterwards, declares the Lord,
his Spirit will be freely poured;
when boys and girls and old and young
will dream God's dreams and
give them tongue,
his prophets speak, his praise be sung.
For the Lord...

Before we see the day of God
the sun turns black, the moon to blood;
'But everyone who calls to me,
and trusts my name, will be set free –
beloved and saved eternally!'
For the Lord...

So look up! See God's city shine,
the mountains brim with milk and wine,
life-giving springs of grace flow down,
our guilt, our grief, for ever gone,
as we adore one Lord alone.
For the Lord...

88888 with refrain Tune: JOEL, by Christopher Hayward

Scriptures: Joel; also Jer 31:12–13   Ezek 48:35   Amos 9:13   Zech 1:3   Mal 3:7
Mark 13:24–27   Acts 2:14–21   Heb 1:1–2
Written: Peckham, Oct 2000
See the previous item; this contribution to marking some of the prophet's main themes was
sung at Muswell Hill in November, to Chris's new tune..

Jonah
Popular prophet; unpopular message

37   IT IS THE LORD WHO SENDS THE STORM

It is the Lord who sends the storm,
to seek for those who run away;
the Lord who gives the welcome calm,
and hears despairing ones who pray.

It is the Lord who sends a whale,
wonders from land or air or sea;
his purpose always must prevail:
it is to set his people free.

It is the Lord who sends his child
to listen, speak, repent, obey;
and if too timid or too wild
he deals with me in his own way.

The Lord gives trees and worms and sun,
to warn or shelter, judge or bless;
strips us until our pride has gone
and clothes us in his righteousness.

In peace or tempest, need or wealth,
in good withheld or new-found grace,
it is our safety and our health
to find the Lord in every place.

One greater far than Jonah came;
life ended, buried, and restored:
Christ Jesus, send us in your name,
that all may know you are the Lord!

LM   Tune: TRURO

Scriptures: Jonah; also Job 2:10   Ps 132:9   Isa 61:10   Ezek 6:7; 48:35   Matt
12:38–41   Luke 11:29–32   John 17:3; 21:7
Written: Bromley, Mar–Apr 2008
Unlike Albert Bayly or Timothy Dudley-Smith, I have not tried to crystallise the main message of all the 'Minor Prophets'. This hymn is a mere dip into Jonah, written under some
pressure to fill a gap. But I hope it encourages us to recognise God's presence, hand, voice
and gifts in some unlikely, unwelcome, even bizarre situations. Is 'Jonah' a mere parable? It
ain't necessarily so…

Malachi 3:6

God does not change; we can and must

38 GIVE THANKS THAT GOD THE CHANGELESS ONE

Give thanks that God the changeless One
can move the earth and stars and sun,
the human heart and will and mind;
the roots of falsehood left behind
to be replaced by what is true,
and all in Christ made clean and new.

Thank God that change is possible,
no evil unavoidable,
no tyrant's grasp unbreakable
nor systems irreversible;
no fault of ours, unmendable,
nor plan of his, unworkable.

Praise be for marvels yet more strange
that even churches can be changed;
entrenched opponents reconciled,
the expert learning like a child,
to gain far more than we would lose
when Christ revives, reforms, renews.

88 88 88 Tune needed

Scriptures: Mal 3:6 Phil 4:2–3
Written: Bromley, and various train journeys, Sept–Oct 2005
This was prompted by two contrasting addresses earlier in 2005. One was a challenge never to accept that 'things can't change', even among nations and even when they seem hopeless; the other, David Hircock's exposition (at Hayes Lane Baptist Church) of the changelessness of God.

Summary: Genesis to Malachi
Old Testament names: a potted roll-call

39 WHEN THE LORD MADE THE EARTH BY HIS LOVING PLAN

1. When the Lord made the earth by his loving plan
he made everything lovely when the world first began,
and to Adam and Eve he spoke his clear word
       but they lived as if they'd never heard.
So they both took from the tree and believed the serpent's lies
and God sent them away from his Paradise;
and the good turned to bad, and bad turned to worse:
       all our race was now under his curse.

2. So these two had two sons, Cain and Abel their names,
until Cain killed his brother and he shouldered the blame;
and the murders went on, till violence and hate
       left the world in a terrible state.
But then old Noah found grace in the eyes of the Lord,
built an ark, and he summoned the creatures aboard;
and the flood brought an end to the rest of the race:
       just eight people were saved by his grace.

3. Later on, the Lord spoke, telling Abram to go
to a land he would live in, which he did not yet know;
he obeyed God's command, God's word he believed,
       and his covenant-promise received.
And then came Isaac and Jacob and all of Jacob's sons;
it was Joseph who ruled all the older ones!
For they all came to Egypt when they needed food
       and the Lord turned the bad into good.

4. Years went by and the people were cruelly oppressed
until Moses was born – he was the boy God had blessed;
he was fished from the Nile, brought up in the court,
       but he had to run off when he fought.
But then God called him to lead, to set his people free;
he said 'I am their God – they belong to me!'
And the wonders and signs of God's mighty hand
       brought them out through the sea on dry land.

5. Moses, Aaron and Miriam and all the pioneers
pitched their tents in the desert for the next forty years;
but in God's promised land they never arrived –
        only Caleb and Joshua survived.
Across the Jordan they went, when God had stopped the flow;
and with Rahab to help, captured Jericho;
but their claim to the land was never complete
        and too often they suffered defeat.

6. With the judges in charge, the good mixed with bad;
and with Deborah, Gideon and Samson, they had
such a mixture of times, of lies and of truth;
        but in dark days the light shone for Ruth.
And it was Hannah who prayed, and God who quickly heard,
so when Samuel was born she gave her son to the Lord;
when God spoke, Samuel spoke; he did not hide a thing –
        till the people demanded a king.

6(a) So then king Saul was the first, until he too went bad,
and the kingdom was given to a Bethlehem lad:
for King David, God had a promise in store,
        of a son who'd be King evermore!

7 But the next in the line was King Solomon;
very wise, very foolish, so that after he'd gone
this proud kingdom broke up and split in two halves,
        and the north worshipped two golden calves!
The sorry tale of the kings is very sad to tell –
so few good ones in Judah or Israel!
Hezekiah and Josiah were two of the best,
        with Manasseh the worst of the rest.

8 Meanwhile prophets announced what God had to say,
with Elijah and then Elisha leading the way;
Amos, Joel and Hosea foretold a great fall,
        but Isaiah was chief of them all.
And as the exile began it was down to Jeremiah,
and Ezekiel and Daniel and the three in the fire;
even Esther had come for such times as these –
        but God's people were now refugees.

9 In our song of the saints we've made such a list!
   What about Sarah, Naomi, and more that we've missed
   such as Job who survived distress and disease?
          What of Jonah's short trip overseas?
   And when the exiles returned with Ezra as their scribe,
   Nehemiah led the building workers tribe by tribe;
   'God is with you!' said Haggai, and like Zechariah
          Malachi preached the coming Messiah.

9a So in the Bible we find each story, every name;
   how they lived, how they died, how they overcame,
   till at last came the One who said 'I am the Way!'
          and this book leads us to him today.

Tune (ironically): A WORLD OF OUR OWN

Scriptures: The Old Testament; also John 14:6 Heb 11
Written: Peckham, May 2001
In her children's work at Carey Baptist Church, Reading, Sheila Stephen (see also no.83) was using a song which listed all the Bible books. She wrote in May 2001 to ask if I could attempt one which took us through the main Old Testament characters in order. Wow! It clearly needed, I thought, a well-known tune which moved fast. Aware that my musical repertoire was a generation or two behind that of the intended singers, I nevertheless fixed on the 1960s hit by The Seekers, 'A world of our own'. In July my first experience of singing it came at Crockenhill Baptist Church which I was visiting for a hymn evening. But they were adults. I am not alone in seeing some drawbacks – but here it is!

Matthew 1
God with us: 2000 years of our Lord

40 IT'S ABOUT TIME AND YEARS THAT COUNT

It's about time and years that count, and moments that have flown;
it's about places, dates and lines, and clocks in every zone;
it's about twice one thousand years since Jesus Christ was born:
    God with us, but destined for a cross.

It's about time to face the truth our calendars proclaim;
it's about Anno Domini – we give the years his name!
It's about time to check out who he is and why he came,
    for his word will show us Christ is Lord.

It's about time to see the hand of God at work today;
it's about time to tune to him, listen and obey:
it's about time to make some space, and travel in his way,
    for he lives, and all his love he gives.

It's about time to search our hearts and change our rebel ways;
it's about time to face the truth in our remaining days,
turning to Christ from worthless things and giving God the praise:
    he has come, and now for us it's time!

Tune: FATHER, I PLACE INTO YOUR HANDS

Scriptures: Ps 119:37 Eccles 3:1–2 Matt 1:23; 16:21 2 Cor 6:1–2 Phil 2:11
1 Thess 1:9–10 Rev 1:18
Written: Peckham, Feb 1999
The London City Mission approached the AD2000 Millennium with the slogan 'It's about time', which it used on its publicity in the preceding year or so. The rhythm suggested to me a catchy tune from *Mission Praise*; although it was sung in various places, we were not granted permission to print it to any other words than 'Father, I place into your hands.' Two composers volunteered new tunes; the whole item may now be past its sell-by date, but here meanwhile is a small piece of nostalgia

Matthew 1–2

Millennium carol

41 TWO THOUSAND YEARS OF SORROW

Two thousand years of sorrow,
two thousand years of joy,
since Mary came to Bethlehem
to have her baby boy:
 Whatever years we measure,
 however many days,
 Lord Jesus, your millennium
 rings all the earth with praise!

These many years of history,
these many years have flown
since publicly at Calvary
a cross became a throne.
 While centuries are turning
 we hear the midnight chime:
 Christ is the Way, this is the day –
 there is no better time!

So many years of terror,
so many years of grace,
since Herod schemed and Joseph dreamed
and Jesus showed his face:
 If time begins in London,
 whatever news is heard,
 inside the dome or nearer home
 let London hear his word!

How many years of goodness,
how many years of wrong,
since fear and gloom outside the tomb
gave way to Easter song!
 The day of God's salvation
 can dawn for us today,
 the Spirit's breath defeating death:
 rise up without delay!

When so much time has vanished,
how much is left to sing
before the day worlds pass away,
and we shall meet our King?
 Whatever years we measure,
 however many days,
 Lord Jesus, your millennium
 rings all the earth with praise!

Tune: THE HOLLY AND THE IVY;
or TWO THOUSAND YEARS by Christopher Hayward.

Scriptures: Ps 118:24 Matt 1:1–2:20 Luke 2:4–7; 23:33–38; 24:1–12 John 14:6; 20:1–18 Rom 13:11–12 2 Cor 6:1–2 Gal 3:1 2 Pet 3:8–13
Written: Peckham, Feb 1999. For the Carol Service at Christ Church, Old Kent Rd, Dec 1999, planned by Helen (who with Jo and John also accompanied its first performance), Jane and Rebecca, and featuring as far as possible carols from every century of the last ten. This was the 20th-century contribution, which they asked me to supply. Stanza 2: 'time begins in London', at the Greenwich meridian; 'inside the dome', Greenwich again – the controversial 'Millennium Dome' across the river but not far from the Old Kent Road. Stanza 1 line 7 can be made more general as 'Lord Jesus Christ, your festival…'

Matthew 3:1–17

The Forerunner and the Fulfiller 1 (see no. 54)

42 ON JORDAN'S RIVER BANK TODAY

On Jordan's river bank today
see John the Baptist stand;
a voice, to start without delay
the work that God has planned.

'Repent!' he calls, 'Come, be baptized!
Turn round, be clean, be free!
A greater prophet, called the Christ,
will quickly follow me.'

They gather, some from every town,
to wash away their sin;
they hear, believe, and soon step down
prepared for plunging in.

But look – who now is walking near?
Is this the promised one –
the Lamb of God among us here,
the Servant, and the Son?

He speaks no lie, no sin he knows,
no law has he transgressed;
his vibrant goodness overflows:
on him God's love shall rest.

With us he strangely takes his place,
for guilt, but not his own;
and soon for us he sets his face
to walk, to hang, alone.

The Judge will be put down with scorn,
the Saviour face the flood;
cursed is the King, and crowned with thorn,
baptized afresh in blood.

From restless crowds to hideous cross,
Lord Christ, for us you came,
brought low, poured out, and risen for us;
all glory to your name!

CM Tune: ST STEPHEN

Scriptures: Isa 53:12   Matt 3:1–17; 20:22; 27:27–31   Mark 1:1–11; 10:35;
15:16–20   Luke 3:1–22; 9:51   John 1:15–36   1 Pet 2:21–24   1 John 3:5
Written: Peckham, 1997–Oct 1998.

At a time when there were few hymns about the baptism of Jesus, I worked on this on and
off for over a year. My starting point was Matthew 3, but its focus is wider than that Gospel
alone. See also no.54.

Matthew 13:44–46 (1)
Hidden treasure; precious pearl

43 HERE'S WHAT THE KINGDOM OF GOD IS LIKE

Here's what the kingdom of God is like ... (x3)
Listen to the words of Jesus:

A man found treasure hidden in a field ... (x3)
and he hid it away again.

He went and sold off everything he had ...
and he went and he bought that field!

Here's what the kingdom of God is like ...
Listen to the words of Jesus:

A merchant looked for beautiful pearls ...
and he found one of great price.

He went and sold off everything he had ...
and he went and he bought that pearl!

That's what the kingdom of God is like ...
Listen to the words of Jesus!

Tune: SKIP TO MY LOU

Scriptures: Matt 13:44–46
Written: Peckham, March 2001
See the notes to no.14: another response to Deborah Woolley's song-search at Walworth, this
time focused on two short 'parables of the Kingdom'.

Matthew 13:44–46 (2)

Precious pearl, hidden treasure

44 LIKE A PEARL OF GREAT PRICE IS THE KINGDOM OF GOD

Like a pearl of great price is the Kingdom of God
when I hear the Good News he makes known;
all his words are like gold, they are tested of old,
and my Lord is the chief precious stone.

He's my treasure in heaven, never earned, simply given;
he's my friend, he's my goal, he's my crown:
Jesus Christ is the prize, and his truth makes me wise;
for my sin his own life was laid down.

Like some rich treasure trove is the wealth of his love,
and it does not run out when we die:
for no wage or reward can compare with my Lord,
and he gives what no money can buy.

Not by luck of the draw nor from points that I score,
but the gift of salvation is free:
I am heir to it all if I come at his call –
come and hear, come and find, come and see!

Should I keep to myself all this fabulous wealth?
No! I'll take it to all of my friends!
There's no joy can compare with this news I can share
and the love of my Lord never ends.

Tune: PRECIOUS LORD, TAKE MY HAND

Scriptures: Ps 19:7–11   Matt 6:19–21; 13:44–46   1 Cor 15:3
2 Cor 9:15   Phil 3:14
Written: Peckham, March 2001
See notes to nos.14 and 43.

Matthew 26:26–28
The Lord's Supper; the Lord's world

45 FOR YOU AND FOR MANY, THE PROMISE WAS SPOKEN

'For you and for many', the promise was spoken
the cup has been shared and the blood has been shed:
for we have been many, the lost and the broken,
but Christ brings the message of life from the dead.

'For you and for many', we tell the same story,
for we have been searched for, and found and forgiven;
The world is so many, so starved of the glory:
so few on the earth for the kingdom of heaven!

With many or few, God is able to use us
in giving, in going, in staying to pray:
whoever comes to him, he will not refuse us,
so let us cry out for the many today.

12 11 12 11   Tune: STREETS OF LAREDO

Scriptures: 1 Sam 14:6   Isa 53:11–12   Matt 26:26–28
Mark 14:22–24   John 6:37   Rom 11:15
Written: Peckham, 1997 and March 2002; revised Bromley, Mar 2004.
Something is lost by those congregations, CofE and others, who never hear the words 'for you and for many' at the Lord's Supper. Our local churches are not alone; the needs, achievements and sufferings of fellow-believers across the globe are often far greater than ours. We are all part of the one body of Christ.

Mark 1:14–15
The kingdom and the King

46 OUR JESUS HAS A KINGDOM THAT IS OPEN WIDE

Our Jesus has a kingdom that is open wide;
he calls us to belong to him, to join his side.
 And where he's King the cherubim sing
 with seraphim rare,
 with angels and archangel,
 all the host of heaven are there;
 the creatures, saints and martyrs
 serve the King of glory there.

Our Jesus who was born a king, a king he died;
he opened heaven's gate when he was crucified.
 And where he's King...

Our Jesus shed his blood for us and many more,
the all-atoning Lamb of God, the Life, the Door.
 And where he's King...

Our Jesus walked beside the friends who thought him dead,
he opened up the Scriptures and he broke the bread.
 And where he's King...

Our Jesus comes one day as King upon the cloud,
and heaven and earth and hell shall shout his name aloud.
 And where he's King...

Tune: KING JESUS HATH A GARDEN / HEER JESUS HEEFT EEN HOFKEN
(Bruges 1609, arr. by Charles Wood), as in *Songs of Syon*, G R Woodward 1923;
and *The Popular Carol Book*, 1991.

Scriptures: Isa 6:1–3 Matt 2:2 Mark 1:14–15; 13:26; 14:61–62
Luke 24:27–32, 44–48 John 10:7–9; 11:25; 18:33–37; 19:19–22
Rev 1:5–7; 5:6–14
Written: Bromley, Oct 2005; first word changed, Mar 2008.
For an old carol-tune known since boyhood, I tried to provide some New Testament content; a year or so passed between the initial idea and the shaping of the text. It remained 'My Jesus', a title used by Catherine Winkworth and Wm Featherstone among others, until March 2008 when I realised how much better is the revised opening; 'The keys of death and hell are to our Jesus given' – Charles Wesley.

Mark 3:13–19
The Twelve

47 FOLLOWING JESUS ONE BY ONE

Following Jesus one by one,
Peter, Andrew, James and John;
Philip, Matthew, Thomas too,
Simon and Bartholomew;
two named Judas, one more James,
here are twelve disciples' names.

Who then were Nathanael,
Thaddaeus, Lebbaeus – who can tell?
Just like Levi, Simon, James,
some had shared or different names.
What counts more for me and you:
are we following Jesus too?

77 77 77 Tune: DIX; or TWINKLE, TWINKLE, LITTLE STAR

Scriptures: Matt 10:1–4 Mark 3:13–19 Luke 6:12–16 John 1:35–51 Acts 1:12–14, etc
Written: Bromley, Dec 2004
Someone (who was it?) suggested a children's song which incorporated the names of the twelve disciples. Not easy; but here it is.

Mark 8:29
Who is this man?

48 LISTENING CHILD OF GOD

Listening child of God,
coming one, who came,
spoken, speaking word:
Jesus is your name.
Breath who tunes our song,
wisdom at our side,
weakness, you are strong;
life, for us you died.

Rock and cornerstone,
link and go-between,
seen and still unknown,
known and yet unseen:
secret, hidden seed,
gift of broken bread;
Israelite indeed,
sign with arms outspread.

Diamond in the dark,
lion, worm and lamb,
arrow to the mark,
evermore I AM:
stem and branch and shoot,
well and waterfall;
tree and flower and fruit,
maker, all in all.

Deeper than our text,
higher than our tune;
questioning, what next?
You are coming soon!
Close, yet way beyond,
far above, yet here:
move us to respond,
for the time is near.

5555D   Tune: VICTOR'S CROWN, by Noël Tredinnick, or new tune?

Scriptures: Ps 22:6   Isa 11:1; 53:2   Jer 23:5   Matt 1:21   Mark 8:29; 12:10
Luke 2:34, 46–49; 22:19   John 1:1,47; 4:10–14; 12:23—24; 18:5–6   1 Cor 1:25–31; 10:4
1 Tim 2:5   Heb 1:2   2 Pet 1:19   Rev 5:5–6; 22:20, etc
Written: Peckham, July 2001; revised 2003 and 2005
This is an attempt to break out from some stereotyped or too-familiar images and titles of
Jesus, while remaining faithful to the authentic record; I cannot now recall what initially
prompted it. Of many Gospel texts to which it could be attached (from Matthew 1:1 on-
wards), one from Mark 8 seems as good as any.

Mark 13–16
Passion narrative

49 NO STONE LEFT ON ANOTHER

No stone left on another,
but every one thrown down;
with brother killing brother
while kings and empires drown:
here is the news, the story
this Jesus has to tell:
the only path to glory,
across the brink of hell.

A perfume-bearing daughter
anoints him for his doom;
a man who fetches water
reveals an upper room.
Another will deny him,
another will betray;
and when they crucify him
all hell is on display.

The cup that he has taken
points well beyond that night;
but then that cry 'Forsaken!'
obliterates the light.
Among us is there any
prepared to call him friend?
His blood is shed for many;
but seems to mark his end.

The women in the morning
have fears about a stone;
the week is hardly dawning
before they find him gone.
But opened is the prison
and nothing stays the same;
this Jesus – he is risen!
He comes, and speaks my name.

By stones and graves and dying
we mark our time and place;
repent, for days are flying!
rejoice, for years of grace!
And while the earth is turning
it is not yet too late;
in Jesus we are learning
the gates of heaven await.

6565D Tune: WOLVERCOTE

Scriptures: Mark 13–16; also Matt 24:26–28   Luke 24:1–10   John 20:1–18   2 Pet 3:7–9
Written: Peckham, Dec 1998
First published: *Spring Harvest Praise,* 1999
A rarity: one of my responses to the annual Spring Harvest appeal for new material which actually made it to the book that year. The morning teaching themes were based on these chapters in Mark's gospel. In 2008 I made changes in stanzas 2, 3 and 5 after TAG had commented; Michael Saward approved the changes but not the hymn itself.

Mark 15:34

That terrible cry

50   SO THIS IS THE DAY WHEN HIS GOD DOES NOT ANSWER

So this is the day when his God does not answer;
how different this hour from the day of Christ's birth!
God spoke at his baptism and transfiguration,
but not when they lift up his Son from the earth.

No legions of angels, but devilish laughter;
no sound from the silence of heaven comes down,
no rescue from friends and no mercy from soldiers,
no last-minute sign and no hint of renown;

but only his thirst and the agonized crying;
yes, only the blood and the gasping for breath.
Completing his work – that alone is sufficient;
the last dereliction, and darkness and death.

So this is the One whom his God has forsaken,
who takes all our sins in his flesh on the tree!
The Lord becomes sin, so that we may be holy;
he dies and he lives for the world, and for me.

12 11 12 11   Tune needed

Scriptures: Ps 22:1–2   Matt 26:53; 27:46   Mark 15:34–39
Written: Bromley, Easter (17–18 April) 2006; revised March 2008.
While preparing a Good Friday service at my home church of Holy Trinity Bromley Common, I was struck by the fact that in the Gospels a voice from heaven affirmed Jesus as the Son of God on at least three occasions, but the 'cry of dereliction' from the cross remained unanswered. Psalm 22 was fulfilled not only in the forsakenness but also in 'O my God...you do not answer'. The testimony to Christ's sonship was left to a Roman soldier. I wrote these lines in Easter week, revising them in March 2008 in response to comments from TAG. They make another kind of 'This is the day...'

Luke 1:26–58 etc
The mother of Jesus: the real Mary

51 MARY OF THE INCARNATION

Mary of the incarnation,
youthful mother of her King,
listening, trusting, travelling, working:
see her wonder, hear her sing!
        O for such a mind as Mary's,
        sharing memory, word and sign,
        quick to learn, by speech or silence,
        where the water flows as wine!

Mary of the crucifixion,
warned of this heart-rending role,
following close where nails and scourges
tear her Son and pierce her soul.
        O for such a love as Mary's,
        costly, pure, enduring long,
        sharing threats and thorns and darkness,
        when most helpless, then most strong!

Mary of the resurrection,
true disciple, Spirit-born:
all her joy is God her Saviour;
blessed is she who learned to mourn!
        O for such a faith as Mary's,
        life that death cannot erase,
        greeting new-found brothers, sisters,
        one in Christ for prayer and praise!

8787D Tune: INCARNATION by Brian Raynor (2006);
ST PAUL'S CATHEDRAL by Paul Bryan (1999); or ALLELUIA by S S Wesley.

Scriptures: Matt 2:13–15,19–23   Luke 1:26–38; 2:1–7,19,33–35,51; 8:19–21   John 2:1–11; 19:25–27   Acts 1:12–14; 2:1–4
Written: Sidlesham, W Sussex, April 2000
First published: *The Hymn* (Hymn Soc in the US and Canada) Jan 2004
With Marjorie's critical help this took shape during our Easter holiday as an attempt to reflect the real, biblical Mary in a text free from fictional or superstitious spin, whether medieval, Victorian or modern. Timothy Dudley-Smith also pointed to some weaker lines which I duly attended to. It was offered to (and accepted by) the N American Hymn Society as part of an appeal for hymns 'to fill the gaps'. Brian Raynor's music was sung by the Kemsing Singers at their carol concert for Christmas 2006.

Luke 2:1–8 (1)

Questions at Christmas

52 HAS NOTHING CHANGED TONIGHT?

Has nothing changed tonight?
 With the months of waiting about to end
 as the praise and pain have begun to blend,
and as Mary's time draws near
will Messiah soon appear?

Is something new tonight?
 When the growing life is so nearly due,
 is he safe and sound? Will he come on cue?
How is Joseph going to cope
with a nation's promised hope?

Can we be there tonight?
 See the tiny head and the eyes shut tight;
 will he one day give to the blind their sight?
Will the name that he is given
be renowned in earth and heaven?

Can we believe tonight?
 Can a mother's mind and a husband's hand
 bringing Jesus up, ever understand?
Can they see the thorns ahead
or the tears that will be shed?

And can we sing tonight?
 When the sweetest tunes that the earth has heard
 are the music matching the angel's word,
and the subject of our songs
is the cure for all our wrongs?

And are we born tonight?
 With the human heart God delights to bless
 finding peace at last in its restlessness?
Yes – it's down to one small boy
who can flood our world with joy!

6 10 10 7 7 Tune: OTFORD by Brian Raynor (2008)

Scriptures: Matt 1:18–25; 2:19–23; 11:4–6   Luke 1:26–45 and ch 2
Written: Bromley, July 2007

This was written for the Kemsing Singers' Carol Service; it was the third such offering for that event – see no.51, the first being 'Dark is all the world below him' from *Light upon the River*. Partly because of its unusual metre it has had to wait a bit longer for a tune, but Brian Raynor composed his in Spring 2008, in readiness for the next Christmas event at Kemsing.

Luke 2:1–8 (2)
More Christmas questions

53 WHAT DID YOU KNOW, SMALL UNBORN GOD

What did you know, small unborn God,
Jesus, the form within the womb?
And did you sense a mother's pain
or trust that good would surely come?

And did you feel good Joseph's strength,
his loving voice and guiding hand
as he, with Mary and their Hope,
was travelling through a troubled land?

Did you then notice sheep or stars
as angels graced that anxious night,
or find yourself unwelcome there
before you blinked to see the light?

Our growing, learning, living Christ,
you have become our Welcomer;
and we your friends, your family,
whose journeys you still love to share.

Grant us your love to drive out fear,
to treasure life at every stage;
the faith to see your hidden signs,
and make each path God's pilgrimage.

LM   Tune: SONG 34, or new tune

Scriptures: the Nativity accounts in Matthew and Luke; also Phil 2:5–11   1 John 4:18
Written: Bromley, Oct 2005; revised Mar 2006
A sense of wonder at the thought of Jesus in his mother's womb, then as an infant, led to
the development of this text which grew in 2005 from earlier ideas. It originally began 'What
did you suffer...', with line 2 using the word 'foetus' which would be more striking but perhaps not easy to sing.

Luke 3:1–22
The Forerunner and the Fulfiller 2 (see no. 42)

54   JORDAN IS THE SHINING RIVER

Jordan is the shining river,
Jordan is the shining river,
Jordan is the shining river
in the early morning sun.

John is standing at the river...
and he calls to everyone.

Jesus steps into the river...
and his work has just begun.

Jesus rises from the river...
he's the Saviour and the Son.

Glory glory, Hallelujah...
for the work that God has done!

Tune: BATTLE HYMN OF THE REPUBLIC/JOHN BROWN'S BODY

Scriptures: Luke 3:1–22; also Matt 3:1–17   Mark 1:1–11   John 1:15–34
Written: Peckham, 1998
A song for Primary School assemblies, enjoyed first at Pilgrims' Way School in the Old Kent
Road – see no.22. It aims to convey a significant story, with simple phrases and repeats, by
a well-known tune. Basic visual aids helped.

Luke 19:1–10

Zacchaeus made slightly bigger

55 ZACCHAEUS WAS A VERY LITTLE MAN / WENT A VERY LITTLE WAY

1 Zacchaeus was a very little man
and a very little man was he.
He climbed up into a sycamore tree
for the Saviour he wanted to see.
And when Jesus passed that way
he looked into the tree
[spoken] and said 'Now Zacchaeus, you come down,
for I'm coming to your house for tea.'

2 Zacchaeus went a very little way
and a very little way went he;
and when he welcomed Jesus in,
some changes they would see.
'I'll split my goods in half', he said;
'Give one half to the poor;
[spoken] And I'll pay back what I've cheated anyone –
and I'll multiply it all by four!'

3 Zacchaeus was a very little man
and a son of Abraham;
and Jesus who can come to us
is called the Son of Man.
He came to look for what was lost
to find and save them too;
and what he did for a very little man
he can do for me and you.

Tune: ZACCHAEUS

Scriptures: Luke 19:1–10

Verse 1 anon.

Extra verses (2 and 3) written: Bromley, October 2005

Born from a desire to reflect more of Luke's account, since the traditional children's song, familiar from CSSM/Scripture Union Choruses, stops well short of its main point. The same thing happens with 'The wise man built his house upon the rock' (What's it all about?); extra lines on application to the author.

John 1:10–11

Faith on the earth?

56 WHEN JESUS CAME TO BETHLEHEM

When Jesus came to Bethlehem, dark was the night;
the world did not know him, though he is its light.
And earth did not recognise the Son who could save,
nor even its need for the love that he gave:
    he gave, he gave;
and the love and forgiveness and healing he gave.

When Jesus came to Nazareth, clear was his word,
and neighbours were stunned at the wisdom they heard;
his neighbours rejected him, closed in for the kill,
and tried to throw God to his death from their hill:
    their hill, their hill;
but it was not the time, and it was not the hill.

When Jesus to Jerusalem came with the crowd
they waved and they shouted Hosanna aloud;
but soon they were calling out a different refrain
and screamed 'Crucify him!' again and again:
    again, again;
and some are still shouting, again and again.

When Jesus comes to London* he comes with no sign,
but brings living water and fruit from the vine;
he comes here to rescue us, to give us new birth,
and this time, will Jesus find faith on the earth?
    on earth, on earth;
and will he find me keeping faith on the earth?

Tune: SANS DAY CAROL; or WHEN JESUS CAME, by Christopher Hayward

Scriptures: Mark 8:12   Luke 2:4–8; 4:16–30; 10:4–14; 18:8; 19:37–38; 23:20–23
John 1:4–10; 3:3–8; 15:1–8
Written: Peckham, Feb 1999
After writing no.41 I wondered if this other 'holly' tune ('The holly bears a berry') might be
pressed into service, also with more New Testament content. This is a more general text –
not just a 'millennial' one; Chris Hayward composed music for this too, but I have yet to
sing either words or new tune. The first line of the last stanza can be adjusted to 'our town',
or with another name etc.

John 1:14
Living among us

57 THE FEET OF GOD HAVE TOUCHED THIS EARTH

The feet of God have touched this earth
and known the feel of grass and growth.
The eyes of God have looked to see
the sunrise he had caused to be.

The hands of God have felt the tree
on which his heart once broke for me.
The mind of God was torn with grief
for our remaking, our relief.

The lips of God have spoken out
in whisper, question, song and shout,
and those with open ears to hear,
receive the message loud and clear.

So, living God, make us anew!
Nothing in us is strange to you.
In earth or heaven, all are yours;
what we have wrecked, your love restores.

LM   Tune: BOWERHAM by Jenny Canham

Scriptures: Gen 1:16–18   Pss 19:4–5; 95:7–8   John 1:14; 19:17–18
1 Cor 3:16,23   2 Cor 5:17–19   Phil 2:6–8
Written: Bromley, Oct 2005
For a couple of years this first line had stood alone in a clip of ideas for possible hymns. In 2005 I at last got around to work on it and sent the result to Robert Canham (URC Lancaster, Hon Sec of The Hymn Society) who had appealed for new items for the next year's conference. His wife Jenny then attached it to a tune she had written for Alan Gaunt's *'Small, like a seed concealed in earth'* and we sang it at Northampton in July 2007. It has been used also at Lancaster (2008) but in March that year I rewrote the final stanza after comments from TAG.

John 1:29–36

Jesus walks this earth

58 HE WALKED BY THE RIVER WHERE THE CROWDS HAD GONE

He walked by the river where the crowds had gone
for the word of the Lord from a man named John;
his path would be taking him where no man trod,
for John said, 'This is the Lamb of God!'
　　Come, see the sacrificial Lamb,
　　Son of the Father, the One I AM!
　　But no-one heard the prophecy of death:
　　they called him Jesus of Nazareth.

He walked into Galilee to shine God's light,
and the sunrise dawned on the people of the night.
He healed their diseases and he raised their dead;
'The kingdom of God has arrived!' he said.
　　Come near, and listen to his word;
　　no-one is like him, he must be heard:
　　and those who come he never turns away,
　　so come to meet him and come today.

He walked to Jerusalem, the road of pain,
and they spat at the king and they laughed at his reign:
they gave him a reed and a robe and a crown;
he gave to them his life laid down.
　　Come, look – he's hanging from a tree!
　　Look in the Scriptures – come and see;
　　to bear our sins he bled and died:
　　but the tomb where they laid him is open wide!

He walked to the hill where the olives grew
and he left us a gift and some travelling to do:
'My Spirit will come, my power will bless,
and you will be my witnesses.'
　　Come, trust in everything he says,
　　turn to the Saviour, and change your ways;
　　you'll always find his promises are true
　　when you love the Lord who has first loved you.

Tune: SHAKER TUNE

Scriptures: The 4 Gospels, including Matt 4:12–17   Mark 15:6–20   Luke 24:44–49
John 1:29–36; 67.   Also Acts 1:1–9; 10:37–43   1 Cor 15:3–4   Gal 3:13   1 John 4:19
Written: Peckham, Dec 2000.

The suggestion for a text to the tune made familiar by Sydney Carter's *'Lord of the dance'*,
but closer to the Gospels, came from Marian Coekin of Southgate and Chris Hayward, then
teaching at Oak Hill College. I admired Carter's writing skills more than his poetic licence.
So while taking a similar theme I tried not to copy his phrases, but to learn from his blend
of quick-running lines with short syllables, and strong beats at crucial points. The 'refrain'
in the music is used here to slip in some more content. Others who had a hand in shaping
this approach included Marjorie, Margaret Hobbs of Southgate, and students at the Cornhill Training Course, where we sang it at Christmas. Among other words in print are *'Tis
the gift to be simple'*.

John 4:1–42, etc
Rest: hours and minutes, then and now

59   AS JESUS RESTED AT THE WELL

As Jesus rested at the well,
some minutes or an hour,
the Saviour's purpose, who could tell?
Who then could guess his weariness?
Who now can grasp his power?

As Jesus rested with his friends
to hear what they had done,
who saw, who sees what God intends?
Who understands that from his hands
there's bread for everyone?

As Jesus rested in the tomb
that doubtful Sabbath Day,
who wondered if his hour had come?
Who now can know how fast, how slow
our minutes tick away?

Lord Jesus, resting now on high,
in kingly robes arrayed,
who can forget you had to die?
Your work complete, your hands and feet
still show the price you paid.

86 886 Tune needed

Scriptures: John 4:4–26; also Mark 6:30–34; 8:14–21; 15:42–16:8 Luke 24:36–40 Heb
1:3; 4:9–10

Written: Bromley, May 2005; revised March 2008.

Originally starting with 'When' and lacking stanza 2, this text on a much-needed theme
seems to require a tune which begins quietly and ends joyfully.

John 6:35, 48; 8:12; 9:5; 10:7–15; 11:25; 14:6; 15:1–8
The 'I AM's of Jesus

60 I AM THE BREAD, THE BREAD OF LIFE

I am the bread, the bread of life: yes, these are the words of Jesus *(x 2)*
    No-one's ever hungry, no-one's ever thirsty,
    if they believe in Jesus Christ.
I am the bread, the bread of life: yes, these are the words of Jesus.

I am the light, the light of the world: yes, these are the words of Jesus...
    If we follow him, we'll never walk in darkness,
    but we shall have the light of life.
I am the light, the light of the world: yes, these are the words of Jesus.

I am the door and I am the shepherd: these are the words of Jesus...
    He's the door to come through, shepherd who has saved us;
    laid down his life so we can live.
I am the door and I am the shepherd: these are the words of Jesus.

I am the resurrection and the life: yes, these are the words of Jesus...
    Anyone believing, they are really living,
    living in him we never die!
I am the resurrection and the life: yes, these are the words of Jesus.

I am the way, the truth and the life: yes, these are the words of Jesus...
    There's no other way of coming to the Father;
    only believe in Jesus Christ.
I am the way, the truth and the life: yes, these are the words of Jesus.

I am the vine and you are the branches: these are the words of Jesus...
    If we stay in Jesus, if his words are in us,
    we shall be growing, bearing fruit.
I am the vine and you are the branches: these are the words of Jesus.

Tune: AN ENGLISH COUNTRY GARDEN

Scriptures: John 6:35, 48; 8:12; 9:5; 10:7–15; 11:25; 14:6; 15:1–8
Written: Peckham, Mar 2001
Mrs Deborah Woolley and other children's' leaders at East Street Baptist Church, Walworth (see nos.14, 43, 91, 92) were looking for new songs conveying some of the teaching of Jesus. Hearing the tune played before assemblies at Pilgrim's Way Primary School in the Old Kent Road, I thought that this lyrical music could be a suitable accompaniment to something based on the 'I AM' sayings in John's gospel.

John 8:54–59
Jesus fulfils all the Scriptures

61 LONG BEFORE ABRAHAM

Long before Abraham,
greater than Jacob,
fulfiller of Moses,
true end of the law;
wiser than Solomon,
buried like Jonah,
and his is the day
which glad Abraham saw!

Praise to our pioneer,
life-giving water,
our passover, glory
and true living bread;
wisdom once crucified,
risen from darkness,
so this is the day
of Christ Jesus our Head!

6565 6556   Tune needed

Scriptures: Matt 5:17; 12:38–42   Luke 11:29–32; 24:27, 44   John 4:10–14; 6:32–33, 51; 8:56–58   1 Cor 1:22–24,30; 5:7   Heb 2:10
Written: Bromley, March 2005, revised May 2005
From some scribbled notes on train journeys, my earlier ideas arrived at this shape at home. Each line of stanza 2 reflects its equivalent in the first; in all, it aims to present Jesus Christ as Lord of Scripture and history, far supreme over even his greatest and authentic forerunners.

John 10:1–30
Christ the good Shepherd

62 GOOD SHEPHERD, YOU KNOW US, YOU CALL US BY NAME

Good Shepherd, you know us, you call us by name,
you lead us; we gladly acknowledge your claim.
Your voice has compelled us; we come at your call,
and none you have chosen will finally fall.

Good Shepherd, you warn us of robbers and thieves;
the hireling, the wolf, who destroys and deceives:
all praise for your promise on which we shall stand,
that no-one can snatch us from out of your hand.

Good Shepherd, you lay down your life for the sheep;
your love is not fickle, your gift is not cheap.
You spend your life freely, you take it again;
you died, so we live – we are healed by your pain.

At one with the Father, you made yourself known:
'I am the Good Shepherd', at one with your own.
You loved us before we had heeded or heard;
by grace we respond to your life-giving word.

11 11 11 11   Tune: ST DENIO, or FORTY ACRES by David Ashley White

Scriptures: John 10:1–30; also Isa 53:5   Mark 14:27   Luke 12:32   John 6:63   Acts 11:15–18; 20:29   1 Pet 2:24
Written: Peckham Nov 2001; revised Mar 2002, May 2005.
First published: *Shepherd Songs,* Selah, USA, 2002.
An original longer version was written for the Church of the Good Shepherd, Austin, Texas, USA, as requested, with an added 'Pentecost' theme. It began 'Good Shepherd, your name is the sign of our church', and the final lines (as published) read: 'Baptized in God's Spirit, confessing God's Son, our church is newborn, our true life has begun!' The version here may be of more general use; in 2006 it was sung at the Church of the Good Shepherd, Tadworth, Surrey, where our grandson Hugh had been baptized.

John 13:1–20

In the upper room

63 CHRIST, GRANT ME GRACE TO LET YOU WASH MY FEET

Christ, grant me grace to let you wash my feet,
and washed, to let them stand or walk or run,
as over mountain, desert, city street,
they bring good news, unlikely victory won.

Christ, grant me grace to wash another's feet,
and count it cause for neither shame nor boast,
nor think some merit makes my work complete
since those forgiven most will love the most.

Christ, grant me grace to follow and believe
in you, who loved me to the bitter end,
learn to receive you, as I shall receive
those you have sent, and those you will yet send.

Christ, grant me grace to live, obey and love,
sent to your world, commanded by your word;
content if you direct my every move,
your name be known, your kingly voice be heard.

10 10 10 10 Tune: MAGDA (Vaughan Williams), KERVAN COVE (John Crothers)

Scriptures: John 13:1–20, 31–34; also Isa 40:9, 52:7 Nah 1:15 Luke 7:42 John 20:21
Rom 10:15 Eph 6:15
Written: Peckham and Cowley (Oxford) Mar–Apr 2002
An attempt to set the foot-washing (as John does) in the context of all that Jesus said on that
occasion. Some find serving difficult; some find being served impossible. The hymn featured
at the Hymn Society's conference in 2006.

John 13:34

The new commandment

64 JESUS COMMANDS US, 'LOVE ONE ANOTHER'

Jesus commands us,
    'Love one another'.
He's the one who loves us
    right to the end.
Anyone can be my
    sister or brother,
or my neighbour
    or my friend.

Jesus has told us,
    'No love is greater,
than to give your life up
    for your friend'.
Even more amazing,
    God our Creator
loves his enemies
    right to the end.

Tune: DOWN AT THE STATION, EARLY IN THE MORNING

Written: Peckham, Sept 2001
Scriptures: John 13:1,34; 15:12–13,17; also Rom 5:6–11   1 John 3:23   2 John 5
Another Primary School assembly song; if the tune is too much of a jingle it is open to others to provide a better one.

John 14:6
Yes!

65 YES, THIS IS THE WAY FOR US TO WALK

Yes, this is the way for us to walk;
sing a song of faith with us today.
   This is our inheritance;
     we are travelling on and willing to
launch out through God's wide earth, by
     sharing in a journey,
     crossing new horizons,
     following the pilgrims,
aiming high for God!

Yes, this is the truth for us to find;
here's an open door for us today.
   Seeing what is possible,
     we are wondering and discovering
all of God's universe, by
     building on foundations,
     meeting fresh surprises,
     serving one another,
making room for all.

Yes, this is the life for us to live;
here's the place for us to be today.
   Free to give and so receive,
     we are worshipping and delighting in
God's sacrificial love, so
     work for peace and justice
     in our generation,
     in the name of Jesus,
Glory be to God!

Tune: SONG OF FAITH, by Anne Greenidge (2005)

Scriptures: John 14:6; also Gen 12:1–7   1 Cor 3:10–14   Heb 11:13–16
Written: Bromley. Jan–Feb 2005; revised April 2005 for general use.
One of my glorious failures, shared with the composer of this exciting tune. We wrote it together for a brand new local school, Bishop Justus CofE Secondary, responding to a request
from the Head Teacher and others; see no.98 and notes. Our original text and tune were left
high and dry, so I tried to make this, the second of our main efforts, more widely useful. Time
for a reminder here that all the music may be obtained from me by any who provide an
s.a.e; see pxiii.

John 18:35–19:6
Another King

66 THE POWERS OF KINGS, THEIR ROBES AND RINGS

The powers of kings, their robes and rings.
  are gone for ever;
resounding names and boastful claims –
  their day is over.

Palace and throne and jewelled crown
  are overtaken
by fire and blood, and sand and mud –
  all now forsaken.

Such was their state this world calls great,
  yet small their merit;
what hope of health or lasting wealth
  shall we inherit?

God's strangest plan required one Man,
  despised and lonely;
he is the way; our hopes today
  rest on him only.

Beneath the sky they raised him high
  in crucifixion;
he paid our debt, whom this world met
  with contradiction.

Yet Jesus lives and reigns, and gives
  love beyond measure;
if we believe, we shall receive
  eternal treasure.

8585 Tune needed

Scriptures: Gen 41:42 2 Kgs 19:13,37 Esther 3:10; 8:2 Isa 37:13,38; 53:3
Dan 5:29–30 John 13:1 John 18:35–19:6 1 Cor 2:6–8
Written: Bromley, April 2008
On a tour 'Through the British Museum with the Bible' led by Clive Anderson and Brian Edwards on 4 April 2008, the occasional half-serious comment was made that 'We could do with a hymn about this'. Here it is. Following soon after no.35, this is the newest composition included in the present book.

John 19:1–37
When his hour had come

67 NOT SO VERY FAR

Not so very far
for not so very long,
Jesus was the star and the song.
But not so widely seen
and not so clearly known,
Jesus wasn't keen on a throne.

None too friendly powers
with none too subtle plans;
Jesus met his hour – what a man!
With not such brilliant friends,
a not too gentle crown;
surely it's the end? Cry aloud! FINISHED!

When the world's in darkness
with a God who fails,
we only see the point of the nails;
but with the flesh ripped open
and the blood gushed out,
can we see the point of the shout? FINISHED!

Not the trend today,
and not so very smooth,
walking in the way of his truth.
But not so very strange,
this dying to be free;
nothing much has changed – only me.

(not finished yet …)

Tune: FINISHED, by Christopher Hayward

Scriptures: Exod 15:2   Numb 24:17   Matt 7:13–14   Mark 14:1–2, 50; 15:12–
15, 31–37   John 6:15; 13:1; 17:1; 19:30   Acts 17:27   2 Cor 5:17   Phil 3:12
Written: Peckham, Aug 1999
Tempted by Hollywood, in the shape of a Californian 'Unisong' competition in which one
category was 'contemporary Christian', I persuaded Chris Hayward to compose a tune for
this and also to gather some Oak Hill College musicians for a recording session, since a tape
was required as part of our entry. But our little effort did not get so very far.

John 19:38–20:20
Friday gloom: Sunday joy

68 THAT EVENING IN THE FRIDAY GLOOM

That evening in the Friday gloom
two men have come to carry him;
they bring his body to the tomb
and make all haste to bury him.

What final gifts shall love afford?
Three women who were dear to him
bring spices for their lifeless Lord
and lose no time to care for him.

But where is he? They cry aloud
'He's gone! What have they done with him?'
What need of spices, grave or shroud?
If only they had gone with him!

Yet Christ is risen – Jesus lives!
We have not far to seek for him;
he greets us all; our hope revives,
and when we find, we speak for him.

He bears the marks of nail and thorn;
what can we think to give to him?
God grant we learn, by faith reborn
to love him and to live to him.

LM   Tune: WOODLEA, by Jonathan Gooch;
HOPE REVIVED, by Trevor Low; or HILARITER

Scriptures: Matt 27:57–61; 28:1–10 Mark 15:42–16:11 Luke 23:30–24:19
John 19:38–20:18 2 Cor 5:15
Written: Bromley, July–Aug 2007; revised Mar 2008
In 2007 David Iliff was preparing a new carol book for seasons other than Christmas, and
asked if I could try an Easter text to the 17th-century German tune HILARITER, with more
Bible content ('a much stronger Easter feel') than other words set to this music. In spite of
some valuable input from Timothy Dudley-Smith, my effort was not quite what David had
in mind, so it remains on file but with two new tunes available, from Baptists in Bromley
and Abingdon respectively.

Acts 12:1–17

His chains fell off

69   SIMON PETER WAS ARRESTED

Simon Peter was arrested,
sent to prison just for preaching
'Jesus Christ, Lord of all!' –
so they locked him up in prison.

But the Christians started praying,
for their brother, Simon Peter:
KNOCK KNOCK! Who's there?
God has answered – here is Peter!

Tune: LONDON'S BURNING

Scriptures: Acts 12:1–17; also Heb 13:3
Written: Peckham, June 1999
It should be clear for what age-group this was written: see no.3 etc. A rather thin text to represent the Acts of the Apostles in this small volume? But how relevant to today's world! A wise leader (of primary school assemblies, junior church, family services etc) can highlight the 3rd line, and find time to point out that not all prayers are answered as dramatically as this. Even where there is no music, the tune should give no problems; singing it as a two- or four-part round also aids the memory.

1 Corinthians 1:13 (1)
Is Christ divided? (1)

70 ONE IN CHRIST – AND MUST WE FIGHT EACH OTHER?

One in Christ – and must we fight each other?
Or be disciples, daring to be new,
in loving God and serving one another,
in holding fast to what is good and true?

One in Christ – shall nation slaughter nation,
rejecting all his kingdom's loyalties?
One fellowship of reconciliation,
or torn by treachery and led by lies?

One in Christ – yet proud of our divisions,
repeating slogans tied to yesterday?
Or finding new disguise for old decisions,
new enemies for whom we need not pray?

One in Christ? If so, then our repentance
can be a unifying bond of peace.
Or on our own heads be it; and our sentence,
that faithless vicious circle, will not cease.

One in Christ, for work and glad thanksgiving,
a cross-shaped lifestyle, worship, praise and prayer,
a harmony of thinking, loving, living;
if we are one – Christ, you are surely here!

10 10 11 10   Tune needed

Scriptures: Rom 12:4–5   1 Cor 1:13; 12:27   Gal 3:28   Eph 4:3–4   Col 3:11
Jas 4:1–3 1 John 3:11–15; 4:19–21
Written: Bromley, July 2007 – Feb 2008
In 2007 the Hymn Society (of Great Britain and Ireland) announced a Hymn Search on the
theme 'One in Christ.' This lent itself to texts which might explore what that means in times
of war – that is, for most of the time. Two English and German Christians, the missionary
Dr Henry Hodgkin and the pastor Dr Friedrich Siegmund-Schultze, were in no doubt; part-
ing on Cologne railway station at a tense moment for Europe, July 1914, they said 'We are
one in Christ and can never be at war'. So was born the Fellowship of Reconciliation (stanza
2), to which I have belonged since 1960. See also no.71. These, I realise, will not receive uni-
versal or even majority assent among Christians; not yet.

1 Corinthians 1:13 (2)
Is Christ divided? (2)

71 WE ARE ONE IN CHRIST AND CAN NEVER BE AT WAR

'We are one in Christ and can never be at war':
words as potent now as they ever were before.
Loyalty to God overrules all human claims;
Jesus as the Lord supersedes all other names.

We are one in Christ, who has founded one new race;
no more slaves to fear, but a people freed by grace.
Vengeance is not ours, final judgement comes from heaven;
ours is to forgive, as we too have been forgiven.

We are one in Christ; enemies are reconciled;
prophecies of hope can begin to be fulfilled.
Do not wait for God to bring peace and justice in;
God still longs for us to renounce our stubborn sin.

We are one in Christ; and his body bears the scars
of the suffering church, not the triumph of its wars;
he provides the signs by the bread and in the cup,
pointing us the way as they nail his body up.

We are one, O Christ! Of your love we have no lack;
Jew and Gentile join, north and south, and white and black.
From one Father God, in one Spirit is our life;
so, one Christ, be ours – by your cross disarm our strife!

12 12 12 12   Tune: KOINONIA by Sue Gilmurray

Scriptures: Rom 12:4–5   1 Cor 1:13; 12:27   Gal 3:28   Eph 4:3–4   Col 3:11
Jas 4:1–3   1 John 3:11–15; 4:19–21
Written: Bromley, 2007
For the background, see the notes to no.70, where the same Scripture references are also given.

1 Corinthians 10:1–12
Warning and welcome

72   ALL BAPTIZED BENEATH THE CLOUD

All baptized beneath the cloud,
all baptized through surging waves;
all sustained by heaven's bread,
living streams from God who saves.

Yet so many meet their end,
live for pleasure, lose the path;
few will see God's holy land,
many fall beneath his wrath.

And is Israel's story ours?
Doomed are all who think they stand,
if we worship this world's powers,
scorn the riches from God's hand.

What a past to leave behind,
what a future lies ahead!
Welcome, all who seek and find
Jesus, risen from the dead!

77.77 Tune: NEWINGTON

Scriptures: 1 Cor 10:1–13; also Ex 13:21–22; 14:21–29; 16:35; 17:6; 32:6 Numb 14:26–30 Ps 95:7–11 2 Tim 2:8
Written: Cowley (Oxford) and Peckham, Mar–Apr 2002
Not all Baptism imagery is that of immersion; we sometimes sing with J M Neale that God leads his Israel 'with unmoistened foot, through the Red Sea waters'! On Marjorie's advice I cut out one stanza from my original five, begun at Marcus and Clare's home during Easter in Cowley.

2 Corinthians 4:6–11

Grief and joy

73 O CHRIST, THE SON OF GOD MOST HIGH

O Christ, the Son of God most high
hear this your sinful servant's cry:
in my soul's grief, remember me;
from heart's deep evils, set me free.

O Saviour Jesus, may I see
your radiant, shining Deity,
my soul and body filled with song
to praise my God all ages long.

LM   Tune: FULDA

Scriptures: Pss 42:1–3,5,11; 43:5   Matt 16:16   2 Cor 4:6–11   I John 3:2
Written: Peckham, 1999

A paraphrase of the prayer by Synesius of Cyrene (c.375–430) which survives in the version by A W Chatfield 'Lord Jesus, think on me' (1876). While Chatfield seems to attribute depression to sinfulness, the revision in *Hymns for Today's Church* (1982) goes to the other extreme in removing any hint of personal responsibility. This is an attempt to stay closer to the original, to Scripture and to reality, also featuring the fuller titles of Christ which it includes.

2 Corinthians 4
Ministry of the Gospel

74   FATHER, SAVIOUR, HOLY SPIRIT

Father, Saviour, Holy Spirit,
God who numbers all our days,
Lord of present, past and future,
help us trace your sovereign ways.

Many years have been our testing,
mountain-top to desert dust,
guided on our global journeys,
toughened for a life of trust.

Many years have seen our trusting,
clothing, shelter, food each day;
through frustration and fulfilment
heart and voice are moved to pray.

Many years have fed our praying,
seeking, finding where to turn;
contrite, thankful, wrestling, waiting –
hidden school where pilgrims learn.

Many years have formed our learning;
studies shaping us to teach,
giving time to search the Scriptures,
words from God to hear and preach.

Many years have fired our preaching
grace we never can deserve;
love from Jesus Christ compels us –
his the Name we speak, and serve.

Many years have spanned our serving;
churches near and far shall sing
at each milestone on the highway
of the servants of the King.

Father, Saviour, Holy Spirit,
teach us how to count our days;
ours the joyful recommitment,
yours the wisdom, strength and praise!

8787 Tune: STUTTGART, or LAUS DEO

Scriptures: 2 Cor 4; also Gen 28:20–21   Ps 90:12   John 5:39   2 Cor 5:14
Gal 1:15–16   2 Tim 3:15; 4:1–2
Written: Bromley, May 2004
This celebrated the 40-year ministry of my oldest friend (from infant schooldays in Brom-
ley) Robert Emery, now in NSW, Australia. Stanzas 2–7 then began 'Forty years...'; other
numbers may also fit, or it may be used more generally in this form.

2 Corinthians 9:15
Gift beyond words

75 THANKS BE TO GOD FOR HIS GRACE BEYOND SPEECH

Thanks be to God for his grace beyond speech,
yet granted to us to receive and to preach.
Silver and gold make a poor sacrifice,
so thanks be to God for his word beyond price.

Thanks be to God for his love beyond thought,
and countless the joys which his mercy has brought.
For new creation the praise is the Lord's,
then thanks be to God for his Gift beyond words,

10 11 D dactyl   Tune needed

Scriptures: Ps 19:10   2 Cor 5:17; 9:15
Written: Bromley, Oct 2005; revised Mar 2008
Like a handful of other short items, this was tidied up in 2005 from some sketchy notes and
further revised in 2008. Its starting–point was 2 Cor 9:15, but I had no tune in mind.

Colossians 1:16–20
All things

76 ALL THINGS IN JESUS WERE FIRST CREATED

All things in Jesus were first created,
everything, everything:
All things – the clear and the complicated:
Christ is King, Christ is King!

All things in Jesus are held together...
All things are under his rule for ever...

All things are his in the church he cares for...
All things – and we are the ones he's here for...

All things are his who is all-forgiving...
All things he gives, and he goes on giving...

All things are his in the earth and heaven...
All things we need we are freely given...

All things at peace at the story's ending...
All things united in praise unending...

Tune: THERE'S NOT A FRIEND LIKE THE LOWLY JESUS (NO, NOT ONE)

Scriptures: John 1:1–3   Rom 8:28–32   1 Cor 3:21–23   Col 1:15–20
Written: Bromley, Nov 2007
Preparing for a 'Family (all-age) Service' at my home church of Holy Trinity Bromley Common in Nov 2007, I noticed the prominence of 'all things' in the set reading from Colossians 1. I linked it with some other notable occurrences of these two words (simply *'panta'*, neuter, in Greek), and thought they would make a sufficiently simple yet positively biblical song. So it was first used on the following Sunday morning. As then, the voice parts can be varied.

1 Timothy 6:6–19
Covetousness, which is idolatry

77   IF THIS IS NOT OUR WORLD

If this is not our world
with all its hollow powers,
to make a god of gold
is no concern of ours.
  The latest gains
  fill all the news;
  we need not choose
  to wear such chains.

If we are not our own
bur purchased at a price,
to follow Christ alone
is no great sacrifice.
  In him, if we
  hold nothing back,
  we have no lack;
  he sets us free.

If goods are not our goal
and all our wealth will rust,
I dare not lose my soul
by scrabbling for the dust.
  Not heaven nor earth
  are up for sale;
  coins are no scale
  of human worth.

If Christ is all our praise,
our heritage, our health,
we need not waste our days
in struggling after wealth.
  And those who give
  their all, and more,
  will not be poor
  but start to live.

6666 4444 Tune: DARWALL's 148th

Scriptures: Dan 3; 5:4   Matt 6:19; 16:26   Mark 8:36   1 Cor 6:19–20; 7:23
2 Cor 8:3–15; 9:7–12   Jas 5:2–3
Written: Peckham, Oct 1998
First published: *First Fruits* (Canterbury Press, Norwich) 2001
My response to a request from Adrian Mann of the Anglican Stewardship Association for 'good quality hymns...which are relevant to the subject of giving, and which do not always avoid the subject of money itself.' With Marjorie's help, this was the final form of the one new text which I submitted and which was included in the published collection, 'a worship anthology on generosity and giving.' Perhaps a new tune would relieve the pressure on John Darwall.

Hebrews 11:8–10

Fresh horizons

78 WE HAVE NOT WALKED THESE PATHS BEFORE

We have not walked these paths before,
nor viewed the scenes that meet our eyes;
what fresh perspectives are in store,
horizons hard to recognise
that catch our breath with swift surprise?

New sounds, new songs excite our ears,
new needs are stretching heart and mind,
unknown sensations, joys or fears;
as passing fashions fall behind,
what words, what wonders shall we find?

And God who formed the ancient dust
and wove the tapestry of space
is far beyond, and wise and just,
yet walks beside us, at our pace,
such is the mystery, such the grace.

This much we know: here Jesus stood,
and finished what he came to do,
for all he did was wholly good
and all he said was fully true,
and what he makes is always new.

For though our knowledge is but small,
our faltering wisdom, feebler still,
he lives, who made and knows us all;
who met our evils, bore our ill,
and beckons from the misty hill.

88888 Tune: FEN MEADOW by Michael Booker (2000);
PORRESHA by Doug Constable (2001); or PACHELBEL

Scriptures: Gen 1:1, 14–18; 2:7   Josh 3:4   Mark 7:37; 9:2–8   Luke 24:15
John 2:24–25; 4:34; 8:40,45; 19:30   Rom 11:33   1 Pet 2:24   1 John 3:5; 4:17
Written: Peckham, 1 January 2000
First published: *Real Hymns, Real Hymn Books* (Grove Worship Series) Jan 2000
While editing the quarterly *News of Hymnody* for a second spell, I invited readers to submit new hymn texts written on or after 1st January 2000, to welcome the new Millennium and appear immediately in our January issue. As the hour approached I wondered if anyone would respond. I need not have worried; but just in case, I completed this text before 7.00 a.m. on New Year's Day. It starts low-key and (I hope) gathers pace and content, referring to the unimaginable past, historic incarnation and present companionship of Christ. Where is the 'misty hill'? Scripture has a few; maybe we each have our own... I was impressed with both the new tunes which were composed; the words were set to the first in *Evangelicals Now* in June 2000, and to the traditional one at the Hymn Society Conference in Dublin in July.

1 Peter 2:21

Christ the pattern

79 IF CONSCIENCE COUNTS FOR MORE THAN MIGHT

If conscience counts for more than might
and justice, mercy, peace still more,
whoever calls us out to fight
we still say No to every war.

If love still matters more than fear
and what seems weak has greater strength,
we shall be called to suffer here,
be widely scorned and mocked at length.

If every person, every life,
deserves our reverence and respect,
at poisoned words fomenting strife
we must protest, we shall object.

If Christ has died, and Christ is risen,
our path is sure, but never smooth;
we trace the pattern he has given,
his way of love, his life of truth.

Each night that falls, each day that dawns,
brings terror to earth's neediest ones:
for grapes have never grown from thorns
nor peace from bombs, nor joy from guns.

So no short cut shall tempt our feet,
for vicious means make crooked ends;
nor shall we think our work complete
till enemies become our friends.

And even if that cannot be
within our span of mortal breath,
we still refuse to bow the knee
to gods of pride and power and death.

If health and hope may yet increase
and seeds of love find space to grow,
our Yes to justice, mercy, peace,
still means, to killing we say No.

LM Tune: ARGUMENTUM, by Sue Gilmurray; or ROCKINGHAM

Scriptures: Mic 6:8   Zech 4:6   Matt 7:16; 23:23; 26:52   1 Cor 1:25–27; 12:31
2 Cor 12:9–10   1 Tim 1:5,19   1 Pet 2:21
Written: Peckham, Apr–Nov 2002
First published: *Songs for Greenbelt* 2003
This text, which took some months in the writing, may prove to be of interest to only a minority. It has been used at various peace events; the paradox is that when all Christians want to sing it, none will need to.

Revelation 4–5

The Holy Trinity

80 FATHER OF ONE HUMAN RACE

Father of one human race:
    Glory, glory, glory!
Sole Creator, God of grace:
    Praise the Lord of heaven!
Rescuer of those who fall:
    Glory, glory, glory!
Source and Guide and Goal of all:
    praise the God of wonders!
    Let all the trumpets sound:
      Glory, glory, glory!
    Shout to heaven, the King is crowned:
      earth, sing Hallelujah!

Jesus Christ the Father's Son:
    Glory, glory, glory!
Servant and anointed One:
    Praise the Lord of heaven!
Hope of nations, hears our cry:
    Glory, glory, glory!
Once rejected, raised on high:
    praise the God of mercy!
Let all the trumpets sound...

Spirit, Spring of life and love:
    Glory, glory, glory!
Breath of God and murmuring Dove:
    Praise the Lord of heaven!
Teaching, helping while we pray:
    Glory, glory, glory!
Speaking to the church today:
    praise the God of wisdom!
    Let all the trumpets sound...

Trinity, our Shield and Sun:
    Holy, holy, holy!
Undivided, Three-in-One:
    Praise the Lord of heaven!
Angels, sing your timeless song:
    Holy, holy, holy!
Saints, your lives to God belong:
    praise the God of glory!
    Let all the trumpets sound...

7676D with refrain; Primitive Methodist tune: COME AND TASTE ALONG
    WITH ME (publ. William Sanders and Hugh Bourne, 1819)

Scriptures: Pss 84:11; 98:4–6; 103:20–22   Isa 6:3; 38:14; 59:11   Acts 3:13 ; 4:27; 10:38
Rom 8:26; 15:12   Rev 4:8
Written: Bromley, July–Sept 2007, based on an earlier text; this version 2 Sept.
Hearing the tune set to earlier words (including 'Blow ye the trumpet, blow'), at the 2007
Hymn Society Conference, John Barnard required me to write a new text for a forthcoming Carol Book for other festivals. For this exuberant music, with Advent embargoed (included in the equivalent Christmas selection), Trinity Sunday seemed an appropriate choice.
The text was settled after much postal debate with John, and a valuable correction to the
structure from Chris Hayward.

Revelation 21–22
Heavenly Jerusalem

81   THE MORNING COMES: NEW HEAVENS, NEW EARTH

The morning comes: new heavens, new earth,
every corruption done away!
Beyond the pain, the promised birth,
creation's longed-for freedom day!
We hear one name dissolve the night,
bridegroom and priest, once crucified;
see new Jerusalem bathed in light,
prepared to be his holy bride.

All joy is here, all death is past;
Christ is our world, our universe,
our Morning Star, the First and Last,
whose blood spells freedom from the curse.
All nations, come! Believe in him
and freely drink from streams of grace,
to share in God's Jerusalem
and find all heaven in Jesus' face.

Tune: JERUSALEM (Parry)

Scriptures: Rev 21–22; also Rev 1:11; 2:28
Written: Peckham, Christmas Eve 1998, revised Jan 1999
First published: *New Directions* (Forward in Faith) Jan 2000
There are perhaps too many texts set to this tune which have aimed to rival or replace Blake's
poem 'And did those feet...'. I had no plans to add to them until Alan Purser, in 1998 Vicar
of Hadley Wood, asked via Chris Hayward if I could write some new words on heaven to
match the familiar music. This text differs from most in placing the word 'Jerusalem' exactly
where it comes in the Blake/Parry combination. Chris, Alan and Marjorie all added comments which influenced its final shape; it was soon sung at Oak Hill, Walworth, Skegness,
Blackburn, Stafford and British Columbia, but not (yet) the Royal Albert Hall. It was mentioned in the Daily Telegraph correspondence column (20 Aug 2001) in a flurry of letters
about hymns and this tune.

LOCAL AND SPECIAL
texts requested or offered for
particular congregations or events

Some of the previous 81 hymns originally had particular places
or people in mind, but have proved adaptable or usable more
widely. The 19 which follow here, and one PS, are more
closely tied to their origins, but included for your interest and
to complete a personal record. They are arranged in approxi-
mate chronological order of writing.

The Cornhill Training Course, Borough High St, SE London

82 THE ANCIENT HILLS HAVE KNOWN HIS WORD

The ancient hills have known his word,
the judgements and the grace of God;
the very ears of corn have heard
where once the Saviour's feet have trod.

If those ears flourish as God planned,
shall ours be dull in these last days?
And if his glory fills the land,
shall we be slow to sing his praise?

From prison cell to open deck,
from tent or temple, boat or home,
through fire and flood, through war and wreck
the Spirit moves, the Scriptures come.

By prayers and poems, dates and dreams,
in journal, parable and song,
surprises, stories, signs and names,
God speaks, and saves, and makes us strong.

So let our ears be keen to hear,
our lips to speak, our feet to run
with news of Jesus, far and near,
from Cornhill, till our work is done.

LM   Tune: WINCHESTER NEW

Scriptures: Matt 5:1ff; 12:1ff; 13:1ff   Rom 10:14–17
Written: Peckham, June 1998
While we lived in Peckham I did some tutoring in the Friday afternoon preaching classes at the Cornhill Training Course, an offshoot of the Proclamation Trust then (and for its first decade) led by David Jackman. In June 1998 some students asked me to write a hymn for their end-of-year celebration. This was it; I had to include corn, hills and preaching the Bible's message. We sang it to conclude a session on 'What Shall We Sing?' but the hymn did not prove durable.

Reading, Berkshire: a Silver Wedding

83   WE TAKE OUR SILVER FROM THE MINE

We take our silver from the mine
our wisdom from the Lord;
for all are his, as we are Christ's
in whom all wealth is stored.

Like silver are his precious words,
refined, unflawed and pure;
today we hear his voice afresh
and know his truth is sure.

When silver is our jubilee
with memories shining clear,
we join with those we love the best
and mark our milestone here.

With wondering thanks our hearts look back
on paths and places gone;
in faith and love we live and grow,
in hope we travel on.

The hand that led us to our vows
and fashioned us as one
still holds and guards, and moves and guides,
through time's unceasing run.

For all in Christ can truly say
'The best is yet to be';
our wisdom, our redeeming Lord,
is Christ eternally.

CM   Tune: CONTEMPLATION or ST BOTOLPH

Scriptures: Gen 2:24   Job 28:1–12   Ps 12:6   Lam 3:22–23   John 9:3; 14:2–3
Rom 5:1–5; 8:28,30
Written: Peckham, June 1999
A Silver Wedding hymn, responding to a confidential request from Sheila Stephen to cele-
brate 25 years of her marriage to Jonathan; see also no.39. Both she and Marjorie helped
with its final shape. It was sung at Reading on 2nd Sept, and on the 26th at Thrandeston,
Suffolk, slightly adapted for the corresponding anniversary for Michael and Janice Mortlock.
I then adjusted it further to make it more suitable for wider use.

West Smethwick Methodist Church

84   TWO HUNDRED YEARS HAVE PASSED

Two hundred years have passed
five generations gone,
since from these pipes were sounded first
the notes which still play on;
earth's history lives and dies
through passing earls and kings,
while wise and foolish fall or rise
Christ's congregation sings!

Two thousand years have flown
since one small handful met,
on fire to make the gospel known,
by hostile powers beset;
like them we long to serve
a people on the move,
to share our faith, to keep our nerve,
and never fail to love.

One all-embracing death,
one high-uplifted Lord,
one rushing wind, one quickening breath,
one life renewed, restored –
this life, please God, be ours,
this Holy Spirit given;
so every voice with all our powers
shall tune our hearts to heaven.

With every note we use
and every stop in turn,
as instruments we sound the news
that needs no skill to learn;
when Christ still calls the tune
what harmony there is!
ascended once, returning soon,
the great Amen is his!

SMD Tune: HIMLEY by William O Jones

Scriptures: Gen 4:21   John 12:32–33   Acts 2:1–4; 4:23–24   Rom 15:5–6   1 Cor 13:8
2 Cor 1:20   Col 3:12–17   Rev 3:14
Written: Lampeter, S Wales, and Peckham, July 1999.
For the bicentenary of the organ of the West Smethwick Methodist Church, by request of its organist (at the
1999 Hymn Society Conference) who then composed a tune for the words. He also provided much local in-
formation; it is possible to omit the first stanza, but a musical theme is required by the final one.

Heswall (1)

85 RING THOSE BELLS! THIS YEAR, EVERY YEAR

Ring those bells! This year, every year, keep God's promises in our sight.
Sing to God! Always, everywhere, each new morning is his by right.
  Hallelujah! Let us claim this year for the Lord;
  Sing God's glory, Maker, Saviour, Counsellor, the Lord of light.

Christmas comes! Let the Gospel in words and actions be heard and seen;
Christ is born! See the kingdom at work where darkness and sin have been.
  Hallelujah! Let us hear the word of the Lord;
  Sing God's glory, by his love made whole again, and new, and clean.

Tell the world! Leave idolatry, end rebellion, seek God's face!
Come to Christ! Join the family, find vitality in this place.
  Hallelujah! Let us give ourselves to the Lord.
  Sing God's glory, Father, Son and Spirit of redeeming grace.

Tune: HESWALL by Linda Mawson

Scriptures: Gen 1:1   Ps 27:1–8   Ezek 37:4   Luke 2:11–14   John 14:16
2 Cor 8:5; 13:14   Phil 1:18, 27   1 Thess 1:9–10
Written: Peckham, Sept 1999
Printed: *Outlook* (Heswall Parish), May 2000
In 1999 Jim Pollard, a retired minister in Heswall (on the Wirral, Merseyside) asked for a feature on hymns for his church magazine *Outlook* and for a 'Hymn for Heswall' for that year's carol service. The parish has two main church buildings. Linda Mawson wrote 4 carol-style tunes, two of which I chose to work with; this was the second (see no.85). As my letter went astray the hymns arrived too late for Christmas, but they were sung some months later and printed in the magazine. St Peter's Heswall has a notable ring of bells; the original opening was 'Ring those bells! This year, every year; brand new century in our sight. Sing to God! Always, everywhere, each millennium his by right.'

Heswall (2)

86 WHEN GLORY SHONE THROUGH THE DARK SKIES

When glory shone through the dark skies
and midnight was brighter than dawn,
then Bethlehem saw its true Morning arise;
this is the day he was born.
> The shepherds believed when they heard
> the news of a child in the night:
> the city of David was home to its Lord
> and the powers of evil took flight.

But daylight was turned into gloom,
and brightness had gone from the sky,
when Christ was uplifted to torture and doom:
this is the day he must die.
> The fishermen who were his friends
> denied him and quarrelled and fled;
> but soon they will stare at the marks on his hands –
> he is risen, alive from the dead!

Come shepherds, come fishermen all,
from fields and from shores of the sea,
come northerners, southerners, come at his call;
this is the day to be free!
> For Christ has come fishing for you;
> there's none that he will not receive.
> Since he is our Shepherd and Fisherman too,
> let today be the day you believe!

8 8 11 7 8 8 11 9 Tune: NEWSTEAD WOOD by Linda Mawson

Scriptures: Ps 118:24   Mark 14:50   Luke 2:4–20; 5:1–11; 22:24–34,54–62; 23:20–
46; 24:6,34,36–40   2 Cor 6:2   John 10:11,14
Written: Peckham, Sept 1999
Printed: *Outlook* (Heswall Parish), May 2000.
See the notes to no.84. This was the first of the two written for Heswall, with biblical and
modern fishermen and shepherds linking the names of the two churches – St Peter's and the
Church of the Good Shepherd. 'This is the day', in each 4th line, is designed to match a dis-
tinctive musical phrase in Linda Mawson's tune.

Eltham College, Mottingham SE London (1)

87 ONE SMALL LANDMARK SET IN LONDON

One small landmark set in London –
here we learn what we can be;
scenes imprinted on the memory,
tower and chapel, field and tree.
Glories past and future wonders,
old traditions join with new;
in this place your hand has planted,
Lord, we bring our thanks to you!

Landmarks line the paths of history
as our God in time arrives:
manger, lakeside, gallows, garden,
set their stamp on all our lives.
Lord, your word shall light our journeys
where your perfect wisdom shines;
now in each new generation
give us eyes to see your signs!

One small landmark set in London
bears its witness through the world;
parents' deeds that shape their children's,
stories etched in blue and gold.
Christ, your sacrifice and mission
set our feet on pilgrim ways;
here spark off our high vocation,
stir our prayer, set free our praise!

8787D Tune: ODE TO JOY (Beethoven)

Scriptures: Ps 19:7; 119:105   Prov 17:6   Matt 16:3   Mark 8:18   Luke 2:12   Heb 11:13
Written: Peckham, June 2000, revised 2004
This is the first of four hymns written for my old school, Eltham College in Mottingham, London SE9. The next three (nos.88–90) were requested; this I offered unsolicited for its Millennium celebrations when Old Elthamians' President Stephen Smith asked me to lead the prayers and added 'One hymn is still to be chosen...feel free to make suggestions.' That was enough; so I wrote this, which proved acceptable then and at subsequent events, with 2.7 ('this unique millennium') revised in 2004 for general use. Some phrases echo the school song of the 1940s, *'Floreat Elthamia'*, words by my old English master C A A Parkinson. Royal blue and old gold are the school colours, pilgrim staves are part of its crest, while stanza 3 reflects the motto from Proverbs 17:6, 'The glory of their sons is their fathers'. Now however we are inclusive as the school admits senior girls.

Eltham College, Mottingham, SE London (2)

88 THIS IS THE MAN WHO RUNS WITH GOD

This is the man who runs with God!
Who aims where such forerunners trod?
He sets the pace, he wins the crown;
he spends his life, he lays it down.

This is the place where he is known;
in China born, at Eltham grown,
the Scotland star who will not fade,
who loves the day the Lord has made.

This is the day, the first and best,
of praise and prayer and Sabbath rest;
for Christ is risen, Christ is ours
for heart and mind and all our powers.

These are the feet that bring good news;
when Christ commands, who dares refuse?
For us he came, for us he died;
be strong; the Lord is on our side!

This is the cost, the body's breath
to love, to laugh, through war and death;
by blood and tears the track is hard,
but untold joy is Christ's reward.

This is the goal, the end of pain;
to live is Christ, to die is gain!
praise God for all whose race is won
and each new life in Christ begun.

LM Tune: TRURO

Scriptures: Exod 20:8–11   Ps 118:6,24   Isa 52:7   Rom 14:8–9   1 Cor 9:24–25   Phil 1:21   2 Tim 4:7–8   Heb 12:1–2

Written: Peckham, January 2002

For the centenary of the birth of the school's most renowned pupil, the international athletics and rugby star and overseas missionary Eric H Liddell. Requested by the chaplain Robert Draycott at two weeks' notice, it was sung at the anniversary service in Feb 2002 and on other occasions, one of which was attended by Eric's Canadian daughter Mrs Patricia Russell. The text touches on many aspects of Liddell's career including his determination to keep Sunday special, his favourite hymn ('Be still, my soul, for God is on thy side...'), and his unfailing cheerfulness through internment in the Japanese wartime prison-camp where he died. Several biographies now tell his story, while the film *'Chariots of Fire'* presented a popular, award-winning but somewhat romanticised picture of his life.

Eltham College, Mottingham, SE London (3)

89 THAT YEAR THEY LAID ONE ROYAL STONE

That year they laid one royal stone,
walls firmly rising on their way,
with wondering thanks, had they foreknown
these hundred years we view today.

Soon, this young school would gather here,
parents and sons with faith and skill,
plodder and star and pioneer;
one with their prayers, we worship still.

Within this place, what music plays!
What Scriptures, speeches, songs are heard!
Space for our silence, grief or praise,
heart-searching thought and stirring word.

Round us, fresh gardens, tree-lined drive,
outfield, arena, stage and pool;
wordsearch and website newly thrive,
science with art to build our school.

And from this chapel, through the world,
sent over land, by sea or air,
God's mission calls us, as of old,
good news to spread, great work to share.

History and hope today we bring
to Christ our royal, risen Stone;
under his cross we serve, and sing!
Your kingdom come, your will be done!

LM Tune: SONG 34

Scriptures: Matt 6:10   Mark 13:10; 16:15   Acts 4:10–12   1 Cor 3:9–11
Written: Peckham, May 2003
See the two previous items and the next; Robert Draycott, school Chaplain, asked if I could write a further hymn to celebrate the centenary of the laying of the foundation stone of what became Eltham College chapel. The ceremony was performed on 18 July 1903 by Princess Henry of Battenburg, youngest of Queen Victoria's family, for what was then a naval college, but soon afterwards the home of the School for the Sons of Missionaries. I found it hard to keep to 6 stanzas, Marjorie rightly insisting that 7 were too many. Several lines reflect aspects of the school's life and history including its long missionary tradition; it was sung at the commemorative service on 5 July 2003.

Eltham College, Mottingham, SE London (4)

90 ONE HUNDRED YEARS ARE OURS TO CELEBRATE

One hundred years
    are ours to celebrate
God's love so great!
      How quickly time has flown,
      how wide the work has grown!
      Our mem'ries of this place
      can all be signs of grace.
One hundred years
    of deeply treasured days:
give God the praise!

One hundred years!
    of service and support,
of work and sport;
      those boys from SSM –
      how much we owe to them!
      Elthamians today
      take up the torch to say:
one hundred years;
    our network proves its worth,
it spans the earth!

One hundred years!
    Old friendships come alive,
new ventures thrive.
      Those well-remembered names,
      those close-contested games,
      each boundary, each pass,
      white line and blade of grass
survives the years;
    in telling of the tale
we never fail!

One hundred years –
    God's word the gospel seed
for every need.
      Our parents learned of old,
      Christ's field is all the world;
      their children follow still,
      find him and do his will.
One hundred years:
    for past and future days:
give God the praise!

Tune: LUCKINGTON

Scriptures: Gen 17:17   Ps 78:1–7   Matt 13:37–38   Luke 8:11
Written: 7 July – August 2007
A hymn for a one-off event only; 2007 was the centenary celebration of the Old Elthamians Association. I was asked for a hymn to sing at the anniversary service, and offered two slightly different versions. After some suggestions from Roger Scopes (Hon Sec of the OEA, the 4th son of missionary parents) to include a bit more about sport (stanza 3), the committee made its choice and this was the result. SSM = 'School for the Sons of Missionaries', its original name. In 2007 Basil Harwood's tune, composed for George Herbert's 'Let all the world in every corner sing', was also a hundred years old. So we sang it in the school chapel for the first and last time.

East Street Baptist Church Walworth, SE London (1)

91 ALL CREATION, SING TO YOUR RIGHTFUL KING

All creation, sing to your rightful King
  who has come on earth to dwell;
Christ the Lord is born! See the new age dawn,
  he is news to hear and tell.
He is Jesus, the Lord and Saviour;
  God is with us, Emmanuel!

On from Bethlehem to Jerusalem
  there are some who find him true;
but in Nazareth they have planned his death
  and his followers are few.
But he gives them his final promise,
  saying, 'Always I am with you'.

Since he loves his own, he must cry alone
  in the garden as he prays;
till the soldiers' spears and the women's tears
  seem to close his earthly days.
But he died for our sins; he is risen!
  He says 'I am with you always'.

Many busy feet pass along our street;
  will they reach where they intend?
Many hearts bear loads on our Walworth roads;
  O, to show each one the Friend
who says 'Come to me with your burdens;
  I am with you till days shall end'!

All the power is his and his word is this,
  though the kingdoms roar and rage:
'To the nations go, make disciples', so
  as we learn from Scripture's page
he says 'Look! I am with you always,
  to the end of this passing age.'

As we share his grace in the market-place,
  by the door or the lions' den,
if the King is here, shall his servants fear?
  Let us hear his voice again
saying 'Look! I am with you always,
  to the end of the age'; Amen!

10 8 10 8 9 8 Tune: ST MARGARET

Scriptures: Ps 2:8   Dan 6:16–23   Matt 1:20–23; 11:28; 28:19–20   Mark 6:1–6; 14:32–43   Luke 4:28–30; 22:39–52; 23:27; 24:44–48   John 1:49; 18:1–3
Acts 17:17–18   1 Cor 15:3–4, 20
Written: Peckham, Nov 2001
By November 2001 we had been attending East Street Baptist Church in Walworth for nearly a year; see also no.91. The pastor John Woolley then asked if I could write a hymn reflecting his chosen theme for 2002, based on Matthew 28:20, emphasising the divine assurance and evangelistic thrust of those verses. I used that verse cumulatively in each stanza, the tune attracting me as unusual but well-known, with a climax fitting the rhythm of the words. Some of these are Walworth-specific; the market crowds, the kiosk door for book sales and open-air witness, the lions' den (Millwall FC), etc. As well as Marjorie, John and Deborah commented on my first presentable draft, and we sang the finished form on the first Sunday (6 Jan) of 2002 with Margaret Brice at the organ. It was used again at times between then and March 2003, by which time John had announced his forthcoming departure and preached at the Thanksgiving Service at Camberwell for Marjorie's life.

East Street Baptist Church, Walworth, SE London (2)

92 GOD THE 'I AM' WHO DOES NOT CHANGE

God the I AM who does not change
    brings mercies ever new;
no time nor space exceeds the range
of One whose grace this world finds strange –
    yet we have found it true.

So Jesus Christ, from yesterday
    through all todays the same,
the same for evermore, the Way,
the Truth by whom alone we pray,
    the Life, the sovereign Name:

From heaven's light to earth's deep gloom
    you brought your kingdom's call:
but for your word was found no room;
for us you faced the cross, the tomb,
    yet triumphed, Lord of all.

All power is yours, our great High Priest,
    to save completely now
all those, the greatest and the least,
who come to God through you, Lord Christ,
    and to your glory bow.

So grant this church you planted here
    by market, street and home,
to preach this truth each changing year,
each week, each day, this grace to share
    and see God's kingdom come.

86 886 Tune: GYLCOTE by Ruth Woodcraft;
or GRANDCHILDREN by Paul Wigmore

Scriptures: Mal 3:6   Matt 4:13–17   Luke 11:2   John 8:37; 14:6   1 Cor 3:9   Heb 7:25; 13:8
Written: Peckham, Jan 2001
By 2001 Marjorie and I had settled in attending East Street Baptist Church, Walworth, where for the next two years we continued to value the preaching, the prayer, the hymns and the welcome. To launch us into that New Year the pastor John Woolley preached on Malachi 3:6; facing us on the wall were texts from Hebrews 13:8 and 7:25. The hymn was prompted by all these Scriptures, and that significant place of Gospel witness at the heart of the lively East Street Market. Marjorie helped me get the text into shape; Ruth Woodcraft, then a church member and organist, composed a new tune, while Paul Wigmore's (published in 1980) remained an option. See also no.90.

Brandon Baptist Church, Camberwell, SE London: a Wedding hymn

93   WELCOME TO THE WEDDING

Welcome to the wedding!
Joining two in one,
God is working wonders –
see what love has done!
Love is found in Jesus,
love to hold and share;
love is found in London,
love is present here!

Welcome to the gospel!
Christ has room for all
from the wise and weighty
to the very small.
Those who know his friendship
from their earliest home
long to bring their neighbours
full and free shalom.

Welcome to the kingdom
where God's harvest grows;
faith for our commitment,
joy that overflows;
far more strength together
than we have apart,
diverse gifts combining,
one in mind and heart.

Welcome to the journey
starting here today,
facing miles or mountains,
we will praise and pray;
building with our neighbours,
travelling with our Lord:
husband, wife, Creator
make a threefold cord.

Welcome to the glory
more than songs can tell;
Hallelujah, Peckham
and in Camberwell!
Bwana asifiwe!
bless us from above:
al Señor da gloria,
for his name is Love!

6565D   Tune: CAMBERWELL

Scriptures: Gen 2:24   Ps 127:1   Eccles 4:12   Mark 4:8,20; 11:22–23   Rom 12:6–13   Phil 2:1–2   1 John 4:7–10
Written: Peckham, Dec 2001 – Jan 2002
Written by request for the wedding of our son Timothy to Sarah Watkins in May 2002, at Brandon Baptist Church, Camberwell – which seemed to demand Michael Brierley's tune, composed in 1960 for '*At the name of Jesus*'. The 300 or so present comprised the largest congregation to date in this 1970 building. Lines 5 and 7 of the final stanza reflect the second languages of the bridegroom and bride respectively; 'Praise the Lord' in Swahili and 'To the Lord give glory' in Spanish. The hymn has been used on other occasions in Camberwell, and at Forest Gate, where Bruce Stokes who conducted the service is now the Minister. Maybe it is transferable after all.

St Luke's Church, Camberwell (North Peckham, SE London)

94 GIVE GLORY TO GOD FOR THIS BUSY HALF-CENTURY

Part 1:
1 Give glory to God for this busy half century
building for beauty and faith in this place;
through all the change in our streets and our scenery,
serving God's kingdom, a sign of his grace.

2 Who now remembers our earlier sanctuary,
sixty years on from destruction and war?
Trouble and grief are still keeping us company;
healing, forgiveness and love, even more.

3 Bearing the title of Luke the great traveller,
doctor, evangelist, author and friend;
honour his name, his career and his character,
taking God's word for the world to its end.

4 Open his book to meet Gentiles, Samaritans,
hope for outsiders and home for the lost;
prodigals, captives, find life and deliverance;
Jesus spells welcome, and meets all the cost!

Part 2:
5 Luke has an eye for the stranger, the foreigner,
time for the children, the poor and despised;
woven with prayer, every page is his messenger,
moved by God's Spirit, and mastered by Christ.

6 Share the great joy of the shepherds at Bethlehem;
Simeon, Anna – salvation from God!
Mary and Martha, Zacchaeus, Jerusalem;
thief on a cross, then two friends on the road.

7 Pentecost dawns, mighty preaching, long journeying,
Philip and Barnabas, Peter and Paul;
prison and politics, shipwreck and suffering;
Good News of Jesus makes sense of it all.

Part 3

8 One in our Saviour, we prize this inheritance,
artistry, music, in circles of light;
space for our praying, to rouse our obedience,
sent far and wide, walking clear in his sight.

9 Give glory to God for this busy half century,
Gospel and sacrament making us strong;
church and creation, praise One Holy Trinity,
God to whom worship and beauty belong!

12 10 12 10   Tune: WAS LEBET

Scriptures: selected moments from Luke and Acts.
Written: Jan–June 2003
Written by request for the 50th anniversary of the post-war rebuilding of the church of St Luke, Camberwell (North Peckham), celebrated in 2004. We often attended and I sometimes preached here, 2000–2003.

The Diocese of Rochester

95 LORD OF GOOD NEWS, AS ONCE YOU CAME

Lord of Good News, as once you came
with wakening touch and kindling flame
come, risen Christ, we dare to pray
to Kentish hearts and homes today!
    Since Justus, fourteen hundred years
    span fruitful peace and battle's fears:
    where saints have worshipped, worked and prayed,
    still is our living history made.

While kings and priests have come and gone
the prophets' warnings thunder on:
throughout our church's fragile days
your cross has stirred our shame, our praise.
    Where diverse signs and stories meet
    in civic square or village street,
    your Gospel brings the best of news,
    your costly gift is ours to choose.

From city's edge to shoreline sail
in constant hum of road or rail,
from castle wall to new estate
one Lord of all we celebrate.
    Where rivers, downland, orchards merge
    with sprawling brick or highway verge:
    by spire or chimney, field or mere,
    Saviour, our thanks shall mark this year.

When landmarks shift and much seems strange
grant us to grasp what needs to change
while humbly, gladly, trusting still
the Scripture's word, the Spirit's will.
    In this rich corner of our land
    in you we serve, we speak, we stand:
    let seeds of glory here be sown:
    through us, your reign of love be known!

LMD Tune: LAMBERHURST by John Barnard

Scriptures: Ps 65:1 Zech 1:5–6 Mark 1:14–15; 5:38–42 Luke 7:1–15; 12:49 Acts 10:36 Rom 10:12
1 Cor 15:20 2 Cor 9:15 2 Tim 3:16
Written: Bromley, Sept 2003 **First published:** *Rochester LINK* (monthly), 2004.
In 2004 the Diocese of Rochester, whose first Bishop was Justus, celebrated its 14th centenary. (The name Justus occurs 3 times in the book of Acts.) Earlier, a hymn competition was announced, and my entry was the first hymn I wrote in Bromley, following my move here on retirement in Sept 2003. It aims to reflect some of the history and geography of West Kent and, with John Barnard's excellent tune composed at short notice, gained honorable mention. It was sung at least at St Peter's Bexleyheath.

St Peter's Barge, Limehouse, East London

96 THEY CAME TO HEAR THE WORD OF GOD

They came to hear the word of God
as now, O Christ, do we:
so bless the teachers and the taught,
by dockland, shore and sea.

They learned the Gospel from the boat
and so, O Christ, may we:
if waves and fishes heed their Lord,
how ready must we be!

They heard their Master's strange command
and here, O Christ, can we
launch out in unexpected ways,
believe, obey – and see!

And one, at least, was penitent:
so may I truly be
ashamed like Simon Peter, then
assured, accepted, free.

O living Christ, what Peter found
let us discover too,
leave fear and failure in the past,
move on to work with you.

Then fishers, builders, harvesters
and shepherds, make this plea:
Speak to our hearts and rule our lives,
our world, our Galilee!

CM   Tune: ST FULBERT or ELLACOMBE

Scriptures: Luke 5:1–11; also Mark 14:66–72; 16:7 Luke 22:54–62 John 21:15–19
Written: Bromley, March 2004
St Peter's Church, Docklands, mentioned in the newer tourist brochures, is not quite what
it sounds. The old St Peter's Limehouse was closed, made redundant, vandalised, burned
down and then demolished in the 1970s, its parish merged with the historic St Anne's (where
I was Rector, 1976–89). As docklands dramatically changed over the following years new
opportunities came, and a barge was bought from Holland, equipped as a church centre, and
formally opened as the new St Peter's in March 2004, accompanied by this hymn which I
wrote for the place and occasion. The then and current Rector Gordon Warren had the
oversight of the project and welcomed the hymn.

Chertsey Street Baptist Church, Guildford

97 BEYOND THE STREET, THE GLORY

Beyond the street, the glory;
hills above the town:
beyond the noise, the story;
cradle, cross and crown.
    The church which God once planted
    through peril, grief and pain,
has found how he has granted
loss that turns to gain.

Beyond the barn, the building,
more than brick and stone,
has held the faith unyielding,
making Jesus known.
    He came to earth to save us
    from sin and death and hell:
his word, his life, he gave us;
God does all things well!

Green pastures, living waters,
spring in every place
for new-born sons and daughters
called by sovereign grace.
    Each name to God is precious,
    a roll-call sealed above
proclaiming, God is gracious,
everlasting love!

Beloved, baptized, believing,
growing in new ways,
Christ's promises receiving,
give him all our praise!
    Beyond the night, the morning;
    the gospel points us home:
beyond the dark, the dawning;
Come, Lord Jesus, come!

75 75 76 75 Tune: PORTSMOUTH

Scriptures: Gen 1:31   Pss 23:2; 30:5; 87:4–7   Isa 61:3   Jer 31:3   Matt 28:19
Mark 7:37; 16:16   John 4:10   Rom 8:18; 13:11–12   Gal 1:15–16   1 Tim 1:15
Heb 11:17   1 Pet 2:3   Rev 22:20
Written: Bromley, Sept 2004
First published: *Evangelicals Now,* April 2005
Requested by its pastor (and *EN* Editor) John Benton, who specified this splendid tune, to
celebrate the opening of the church extension – a new landmark in its growth and develop-
ment in 2005. According to a current railway magazine read on the Portsmouth train, Guild-
ford presents 'The best of both worlds'. The church began in a barn and endured much
persecution; these and other aspects of its history are touched on here.

Bishop Justus Church of England Secondary School, Bromley Common

98 COME WITH US TO SING NEW SONGS

Come with us to sing new songs
  of faith and hope and joy;
move to the beat of truth and love
  that time cannot destroy.
    Building a school together,
    firm on the sure foundation stone,
let Bishop Justus rise up tall today!

Come with us to bring new gifts
  and talents we can share,
making the time to listen, and
  exchanging help or care.
    Music and art and science,
    learning and living, sport and skill,
enrich our praise and worship here today.

Come with us to make new space
  where everyone belongs;
fairness and freedom, true respect,
  reflected in our songs.
    Whether it's hard or easy,
    happy or hurting, weak or strong,
for one another, give God thanks today!

Come with us to walk new ways
  with confidence and grace;
Christ is the Lord who walks with us
  and sets the perfect pace.
    Treasuring town and country,
    pilgrims along the path, we find
undreamed horizons open up today.

Come with us to climb new heights
  of wonders to explore,
taking the risks to shape the kind
  of world we're longing for.
    Spirit of God, be with us,
    blessing our school, to give us life
to spread through us and all the world today!

Tune: BISHOP JUSTUS by Anne Greenidge (2005)

Scriptures: Ps 96:1 Rom 8:11 1 Cor 3:9–11; 13:13 1 Thess 5:12–18 1 Pet 4:10
Written: Bromley, Jan–Feb 2005
Half a mile from my home, this new school was opened in 2004 and its buildings formally dedicated a year later. I was asked by the Head Teacher and others to write words for a school hymn or song, with Anne Greenidge as composer. Together we produced two very different works, stately/traditional and lively/jazzy. While both were approved, we were asked to try again and this was the result. It was acclaimed with enthusiasm by groups of both staff and pupils, then sung once or twice more before sinking without trace. Justus was the first Bishop of Rochester when the Diocese was founded in 604; 2004 marked its first 1400 years See also nos.65 and 95.

Pilgrim Homes for elderly Christians

99 GOD OF FRESH DISCOVERIES

God of fresh discoveries,
tiny cells to furthest space,
thank you for your earth and skies;
and this house, this special place.

God of centuries now past,
Lord of unknown years to come,
guide us, Saviour, till at last
all the ransomed reach their home.

God of quietness and peace,
calm and rest and Sabbath day,
thank you for the silences,
time to ponder and to pray.

God of sound and music's flow,
grant to our community
songs of now and long ago
in the Spirit's unity.

God whose mercy never ends,
found in neighbours' loving care,
thank you for our dearest friends;
in our need, they will be there.

God whose Son endured the cross,
for our sake becoming poor,
for your love poured out for us,
praise and glory evermore!

7777 Tune: BUCKLAND or LÜBECK.
or as 3 verses of 7777D to SALZBURG or ST EDMUND

Scriptures: Isa 35:10 Mark 2:27 Rom 5:5 2 Cor 5:8; 8:9 Eph 4:3; 5:18–20 Heb 12:2; 13:20
Written: Bromley, June–Aug 2006, revised Mar 2008
First published: *Pilgrim Hymns,* 2007
The Pilgrim Homes were founded by Baptists in 1807 to provide residential care for elderly Christians. In 2006 several hymnwriters were invited to submit texts for a small bicentenary collection of new hymns set to familiar tunes. Together with nos.4 and 24, this was accepted for the book, which was launched with the 2007 celebrations. This one seems more specific than the others to its original purpose; hence its placing here. It was TAG who in 2008 preferred the text to be arranged in six 4-line verses.

Church of the Holy Redeemer, Streatham, South London

100   WHEN ABRAHAM AT SEVENTY-FIVE

When Abraham at seventy-five
is told 'Get up and go!'
he knows the voice that speaks, but not
the land that God will show.

He hears the promise from the Lord
to bless him on his way,
and he will be a blessing too
for many from that day.

With all his household he sets out
in swift obedient faith;
he marks a place to worship God,
the Lord of all the earth.

So bless this household, mighty God
who made us yours by grace;
Holy Redeemer, let us be
a blessing in this place!

For seventy-five historic years
we owe you thanks and praise;
keep us obedient to your word
and faithful in your ways.

As we make space to worship, serve,
and learn from Scripture's page,
your Gospel sets our future course,
built in at every stage.

So fill our hearts with love for Christ
who came to free the slaves
from sin, and death, and wrath to come;
he died, he lives, he saves!

CM   Tune: AMAZING GRACE (thoughtful) or ST STEPHEN (brisker)

Scriptures: Gen 12:1–7; also John 8:31–39   Acts 13:38–39   Rom 8:1–2   Gal 5:1
1 Pet 2:16
Written: Bromley, March 2007
Specifically for the Church of the Holy Redeemer, Streatham, S London, where I preached
several times from 2005 onwards at the invitation of the vicar Ian Gilmour. 2007 was not
only the church's 75th birthday year but also the 200th anniversary of the abolition of slavery in the British Empire. The aptly-named church (see stanza 4) was founded in commem-
oration of William Wilberforce and the 'Clapham Sect'. Both kinds of slavery were strikingly
referred to by Christopher Ash, addressing a large celebration there in March that year.

Appendix 1

Matthew 27:33
Golgotha

THE PLACE TOOK ITS NAME FROM A SKULL

The place took its name from a skull
and the field took its name from some blood:
but the name of the city is peace
and the man took his name from his God.

On Golgotha men put a cross:
Akeldama was Judas's grave:
and Jerusalem, scene of Shalom,
is where Jesus proved mighty to save.

Whatever this world cares to think
and whatever new titles it gives,
still the text of our story is grace,
saying 'Everyone lives, who believes!'

Whoever we are, or have been
and whatever our place or our name,
still our need is the same as it was
and the pathway to peace, still the same.

8999   Tune: CELESTE; or tune needed

Scriptures: Ps 122:6–9   Isa 63:1   Matt 23:37; 27:33–35   Mark 15:22
Luke 13:34; 19:41–42   John 3:15; 6:47; 11:25; 14:27; 19:17–18   Acts 1:15–19
Rom 5:1
Written: London–Cardiff March 2004
An exercise in Bible place-names, or something more? Much may depend on the tune. I am often uneasy about the weight placed on the word 'Calvary' in evangelical tradition, including hymns. Is it just the English rhyme which denies 'Golgotha' similar treatment and affection? A train journey to Cardiff allowed me to put some ideas on paper. Some friends awarded this the celebrated 'nul points' (readable, not singable); others thought we sometimes need the jolt that this may give. So I place it here as my first 'special case'.

Appendix 2

The Metropolitan Tabernacle,
Elephant and Castle, SE London

LOOK UNTO ME AND BE YE SAVED

'Look unto Me and be ye saved
Ye ends of all the earth!'
God gave the word, so we believed;
From heaven came our birth.

'Look unto Me and be ye saved!'
God's Son for sin atoned;
His blood was shed, his work achieved,
His enemies dethroned.

'Look unto Me and be ye saved!'
The elect he sets apart,
His word of truth is now engraved
Upon their mind and heart.

'Look unto Me and be ye saved!'
No God is there but One:
One Lord obeyed, one faith received,
One baptism undergone.

'Look unto Me and be ye saved!'
The ends of earth have come;
All nations in their crimes depraved
Find pardon, rest and home.

'Look unto Me and be ye saved!'
The very stones will shout;
If truth is from these walls perceived,
Much more shall we cry out!

As tens of thousands pass this place
By earthly toils enslaved,
Let all now seek the throne of grace:
'Look unto Me – be saved!'

CM   Tune: NATIVITY

Scriptures: Isa 45:22   Luke 19:40   John 3:3–8   Rom 3:22–26   Eph 4:5–6
Heb 4:18   1 Pet 1:1–2
Written: Peckham, July–Sept 2001
A curio of curios; offered to a church where I valued the preaching of its pastor Dr Peter Masters (with whom I found much common ground when we met), but not its unreformed stance on the language of prayer and praise. This is framed in the archaic style then in use (see 1 Cor 9:22), and built on the prominently displayed words of Isaiah 45:22(AV) which was instrumental in the famous conversion of the church's founder, Charles Haddon Spurgeon.

Appendix 3: altered or corrected texts

Some hymn texts have needed alterations since they were first published, or have sometimes been misprinted. Where the text varies from that in *Light upon the River*, the authentic version is given here:

Ascended Christ
2.7   of worth or fame

Baptized into Christ Jesus
1.5–6   Then just as Christ is risen
                       through God the Father's power,

How clear and true the skies sing out God's praise
5.4   my Rock, my strong Redeemer, and my Lord.

I love you , O Lord, you alone
1.1   Strong Lord, let me love you alone.

If Christ had not been raised from death
3.6   through him we are restored:

In you, O Lord, I find my refuge
3.8   come now with mercies from above.
4.1   For those who fear you, such great goodness,

Light of gladness, Lord of glory
1.3   shine among us in your mercy

Listen, my friends, to each word
8.2   and the maidens had no wedding song:

Lord, to you we lift our voices
1.5   heart's desires, heartfelt prayers,

Lord, you sometimes speak in wonders
4.1   Lord, you love to speak in Scripture

My heart is ready, O my God
7.2   when facing stubborn wrong!

My heart rejoices and my strength is kindled
1.4   none like the Lord, my Rock.

Now is the time, the time of God's favour

1.3   let us repent, and turn back to the Saviour

O Lord whose love designed this day

4.1   But now we see your wounded hands;

5.1   So through the darkness, be our light

Powerful in making us wise to salvation

3.4   these are the Scriptures: on them we rely.

Then I saw a new heaven and earth

2.3   there'll be no more crying or grief or pain;

5.1   And I saw by the sacred throne

5.3   and the tree of life with its healing leaves

To God our strength come, sing aloud

6.5   I would have given you finest wheat,

Towering over road and river

2.2   of our joys and tears

Up from the depths I cry to God

Stanza 2   If you, my God, should measure guilt,
then who stands free from blame?
But true forgiveness comes from you;
we trust, and fear your name.

When lawless people thrive

1.7   the justice of your righteous cause

When this land knew God's gracious love outpoured

1.3   then was turned back the anger of the Lord,

Wise men, they came to look for wisdom

1.6   wealth and redemption, life and love.

INDEX OF SCRIPTURES
selected references only

Bible text:	Hymn no:
OLD TESTAMENT	39
Genesis	
1–3	1
1:1	78, 85
1:14–18	78
1:16–18	57
1:24–25	2
1:31	2, 97
2–3	3
2:7	78
2:19–20	2
2:24	83, 93
3:17	2
4:21	84
12:1–7	65, 100
17:1–18:15	4
17:17	90
28:20–21	74
Exodus	
2–4	5
2:24	19
3:1–15	6
7	5
11–15	5
14:21–22	4
15:19–21	4
19:3–6	21
20:1–17	7
20:8–11	88
Deuteronomy	
4:5–21	7
6:4–5	7
Joshua	
3:4	78
11:23	8

1 Samuel	
14:6	45
17:1–50	9
1 Kings	
1–11	10
3:4–15	11
2 Kings	
19:13, 37	66
1 Chronicles	
29:21–25	10
2 Chronicles	
1:1–12	11
Ezra	
7:6–10	12
Nehemiah	
8	12
Esther	
3:10	66
8:2	66
Job	
28:1–12	83
Psalms	
1	13
12:6	83
19:7	87
19:7–11	14, 44
19:10	75
22:1–2	50
22:16	25
23:2	97

37:7	15
42:1–3,5,11	73
43:5	73
55:9–11	25
62	15
78:1–7	90
87:4–7	97
90:12	16, 74
95:3–4	33
96:1	98
98:4–6	80
99:1	29
102	17
103:20–22	80
109	18
111	19
117	20
118:24	41, 88
119:105	14, 87
122:6–9	App 1
127:1	93
132:9	37
135	21
Proverbs	
1:1–7	10
17:6	87
Ecclesiastes	
3:1–2	40
4:9–12	22
4:12	93
Isaiah	
1–12	23
6:1–3	46
6:1–8	32
6:3	80
11:1	48

35:10	99
45:22	App 2
46:4	24
52:7	88
53:11–12	44
61:3	97
61:10	37

Jeremiah

17:5–8	13
31:12–13	35

Ezekiel

48:35	25, 36, 37

Daniel

1–6	27
3	77
5:4	77
5:29–30	66
6:16–23	91
7	28
7–12	29
7:13–14	27
8	30
9	31
10	32
11	33
12	34
12:3	27

Joel

(whole book)	35, 36

Jonah

(whole book)	37

Micah

6:8	79

Zechariah

1:5–6	95
4:6	79

8:1–5	25

Malachi

3:6	38, 92
3:7	36

NEW TESTAMENT

The Four Gospels	58

Matthew

1	40, 53
1:18–25	52
1:20–23	91
1:21	48
1:23	40
2:2	46
2:1–20	41, 53
2:13–15	51
2:19–23	51, 52
3:1–17	42
4:12–17	58
5:17	61
6:19	77
6:19–21	14, 44
6:33	30
7:13–14	67
7:16	79
10:1–4	47
11:28	15, 91
12:38–41	37
12:38–42	61
12:42	10
13:37–38	90
13:44	14
13:44–46	43, 44
23:37	25
24:26–28	49
26:26–28	45
26:52	79
26:53	50
27:27–31	42
27:33	App 1
27:46	50

27:57–61	68
28:1–10	68
28:19–20	91, 97

Mark

1:1–11	42, 54
1:14–15	46, 95
3:13–19	22, 47
6:30–34	59
7:37	78, 97
8:12	56
9:2–8	78
11:22–23	93
12:10	48
12:28–31	7
13–16	49
13:7–10	34
13:10	89
13:24–27	28, 36
14:22–24	45
14:50	86
14:61–62	28, 46
15:6–20	58
15:22	App 1
15:34–39	50
15:42–16:8	59, 68
16:16	97

Luke

(whole book)	94
1:4–25	4
1:26–38	51
1:57–79	4
1:68	19
2	51, 52, 53
2:4–7	41
2:4–8	56
2:4–20	86
2:11–14	85
2:12	87
2:25–38	4
2:34	48
3:1–22	42

4:16–30	56	8:34–36	1	**Romans**	
5:1–11	86, 96	8:56–58	61	5:5	99
6:12–16	47	10:1,14	86	5:6–11	64
7:42	63	10:1–30	62	5:12–21	3
8:11	90	10:7–9	46	8:1–2	100
9:51	42	10:7–15	60	8:11	98
11:29–32	37, 61	11:25	46, 60, App 1	8:18	97
12:49	95	13:1	64, 66	8:19–21	2
19:1–10	55	13:1–20	63	8:26	80
19:37–38	56	13:34	64	8:28–32	76
19:40	App 2	14:6	39, 41, 60, 65	10:14–17	82
19:41–42	25	15:1–8	56, 60	12:4–5	70, 71
21:9–11	30	15:12–13	64	12:6–13	93
23:20–23	56	18:33–37	46	13:11–12	41, 97
23:20–46	86	18:35–19:16	66	14:8–9	88
23:30–24:19	68	19:17–18	57	15:5–6	84
24:1–10	41, 49	19:19–22	46		
24:15	78	19:25–27	51	**1 Corinthians**	
24:36–40	59, 86	19:30	67, 78	1:13	70, 71
24:39	25	19:38–20:18	68	1:25–31	48
24:44–49	58	20:1–18	41, 49	3:9	92
		21:7	37	3:9–11	89, 98
John		21:15–19	96	3:10–14	65
1:1	48			4:6–11	73
1:1–3	76	**Acts**		5:7	61
1:4–10	56	(whole book)	94	7:23	77
1:14	57	1:1–9	58	9:24–25	88
1:15–36	42	1:12–14	47, 51	10:1–4	5
1:29–36	58	1:15–19	App 1	10:1–13	72
2:1–11	51	1:15–26	18	10:4	48
2:18–22	10	2:1–4	84	12:27	70, 71
3:15	App 1	2:14–21	35, 36	13:12	24
4:4–26	59	4:10–12	89	13:13	98
4:10	97	4:27	80	15:3–4	58
4:10–14	48, 61	10:36	95	15:45–49	3
4:34	78	10:37–43	58		
5:22	35	10:38	80	**2 Corinthians**	
5:28–29	34	12:1–17	69	1:20	84
5:39	74	17:24–31	33	4	74
6:32–33	61	17:26	3	4:1	32
6:35	60	17:30–31	1	5:14	74
8:12	60			5:15	31, 68
8:31–39	100			5:17	67, 75

6:1–2	16, 40, 41	**Hebrews**		4:19	58
8:3–15	77	1:1	29		
8:9	99	1:2	48	**Revelation**	
9:7–12	77	1:3	59	1:5–7	28, 46
9:15	75, 95	1:10–12	17	1:11	81
12:9–10	79	4:9–10	59	2:28	81
		4:12	12	3:14	84
Galatians		4:14–16	31	4:8	80
1:15–16	74, 97	7:25	92	5:5–6	48
3:28	70, 71	11	39	12:7–9	34
5:1	100	11:13	87	21:1	35
5:13–14	7	11:13–16	65	21–22	81
		11:36–40	33	21:20	48
Ephesians		12:1–2	4, 21, 88	22:20	97
3:20	11	12:2	99		
4:3	99	12:22–25	12, 21		
4:5–6	App 2	12:28	28		
5:18–20	99	13:3	69		
		13:8	17, 92		
Philippians					
1:21	88	**James**			
1:27	85	1:12	14		
2:1–2	93	1:17	24		
3:12–14	14	4:1–3	8, 70, 71		
4:4	20	5:2–3	77		
Colossians		**1 Peter**			
1:15–20	76	1:1–2	App 2		
3:12–17	84	1:4	14		
		2:9–10	21		
1 Thessalonians		2:16	100		
1:9–10	40, 85	2:21	79		
5:12–18	98	2:21–24	42		
		2:24	62, 78		
1 Timothy		4:10	98		
1:5,19	79				
1:15	97	**2 Peter**			
2:5	48	1:19	48		
		1:19–20	29		
2 Timothy		3:7–9	49		
3:15	74				
3:16	95	**1 John**			
4:1–2	74	3:2	73		
4:7–8	88	4:7–10	93		

INDEX OF THEMES

*selected: from texts and
titles, but not from all the notes; omitting items
which occur repeatedly (praise, prayer etc).*

Aaron 4, 39
Abel 39
Abraham 4, 39,
    55, 61, 100
Adam 2, 3, 39
Akeldama App 1
Amos 39
Andrew 47
angels 21, 46,
    50, 52, 53, 80
Anna 4, 94
anniversaries 16, 83,
    84, 88–90, 94, 95, 100
art 89, 94, 98
atonement 1, 23, 42,
    46, 50, 58, 66, App 2

baptism 42, 72,
    97, App 2
baptism of Jesus 42,
    50, 54
Barnabas 94
Bartholomew 47
beauty 2, 25, 35, 39, 94
bells 85
Bethlehem 39, 41,
    56, 86, 91, 94
Bible (see also Scripture,
    word of God) 39
blood 5, 36, 66,
    88, App 1
blood of Christ 42, 45,
    46, 49, 50,
    67, 81, App 2
bread 26, 46,
    48, 59–61, 71, 72
Bromley Common 98

builders, building 17,
    39, 65, 89,
    93, 94, 96–98
burial of Jesus 37, 61, 68

Cain 39
Caleb 39
Calvary 35, 41
Camberwell 93, 94
change 38, 40,
    52, 58, 92, 94, 95
cherubim 46
children (as subject) 8, 17,
25, 36, 39, 56, 87, 90, 94
children's items
(and all-age events) 3, 6,
9, 14, 22, 39, 43, 47, 54,
55, 60, 64, 65, 69, 76
China 88
Christmas 52, 53, 85, 86
city, cities 12, 17,
    25, 26, 36, 63, 91, 95
confession 31
conscience 79
Cornhill Training
    Course 82
covenant 5, 12,
    19, 31, 39
creation 1–3, 10,
    37, 39, 76, 78, 80, 91
creatures, animals 2,
    30, 39, 46
cup 45, 49, 71

Daniel 27–34, 39
David 9, 10, 39, 86
Day of the Lord 35, 36

Deborah 39
desert (noun) 5, 6,
    39, 63, 74
devil 39
disciples (see also twelve)
    46, 47, 51, 70, 91
dockland 96
dreams 25, 27,
    29, 35, 36, 41, 82
dust 17, 19, 34,
    74, 77, 78

Easter 16, 41
Eden 2
Egypt 21, 39
Elijah 39
Elisha 39
Elizabeth 4
Eltham College 87–90
enemies 17, 18, 64, 70,
    71, 79, App 2
Esther 39
Eve 3, 39
evening 68
exile 27, 31, 39
exodus 4–7, 19, 21, 39
Ezekiel 39
Ezra 12, 39

faithfulness of God 20
fasting 32
fire and cloud 5
fishermen 86, 96
flood 39, 82
following Jesus 1,
    25, 47, 60, 63, 77

freedom, liberty 1, 7, 12, 17, 35–37, 39, 71, 73, 81, 96, 98, 100
friendship   44, 46, 53, 59, 64, 79, 86, 90, 93, 94, 99

Gabriel   30
Galilee   58, 96
garden(s)   3, 87, 89, 91
Gentiles   71, 94
Gideon   39
gifts, talents   10, 93, 98
Golgotha   App 1
Goliath   9
good, goodness   11, 13, 15, 21, 36, 39, 41, 42, 53, 62, 70, 78
good news 1, 33, 44, 63, 88, 89, 94, 95
gospel 1, 24, 33, 35, 84, 85, 90, 93, 95–97, 100
gratitude,
see thanksgiving
Guildford   97

Haggai   39
Hannah   39
harvest   16, 36, 93, 96
healing   18, 58, 62, 94
Herod the Great   41
Heswall   85, 86
Hezekiah   39
hill, hills   4, 16, 17, 21, 56, 58, 78, 82, 97
history   28, 39, 40, 84, 87, 89, 90, 95, 97, 99
Hosea   39
hospitals   8

idolatry   7, 21, 23, 27, 33, 39, 72, 77, 79, 85
incarnation   40, 51–53, 57, 78

insects   2, 10, 35–36
Isaac   39
Isaiah   32, 39
Israel   11, 21, 31, 32, 39, 72

Jacob   21, 39, 61
James (son of Zebedee)47
James (son of Alphaeus)
                  47
Jeremiah   39
Jericho   39
Jerusalem 17, 21, 56, 58, 81, 91, 94, App 1
Jews   71
Job   39
Joel   35–36, 39
John (disciple)   47
John the Baptist   42, 54, 58
Jonah   37, 39, 61
Jordan   39, 42, 54
Joseph (OT)   39
Joseph (NT)   41, 52, 53
Joshua   39
Josiah   39
Judah   39
Judas   47
Judas Iscariot   18, 47, App 1
judgement, wrath 1, 5, 7, 13, 18, 23, 28, 33–35, 71, 72
judges   39
justice 23, 65, 71, 78, 79
Justus, Bishop   95, 98

Kent   95
kingdom of God/
Christ/heaven   10, 14, 27, 28, 43, 44, 46, 58, 85, 89, 92–94
kings   10, 11, 15, 21, 27–29, 39, 49, 66, 84, 95

landmark(s)   87, 95
Lebbaeus   47
Levi (Matthew?)   47
Levites   12
Liddell, Eric   88
Limehouse   96
London 41, 56, 87, 91–94, 96, 100, App 2
Lord's Day   16, 88
Lord's Supper, Holy
   Communion 26, 45, 71
Luke   94

Malachi   39
Manasseh   39
market, market-place
                  91, 92
marriage   7, 83, 93
Martha   94
martyrs   46
Mary, mother of Jesus
                  41, 51–53
Mary of Bethany   94
Matthew   47
Metropolitan Tabernacle
                  App 2
Michael
   (archangel)   34, 46
milestone   74, 83
milk   36
millennium (AD2000)
                  40, 41, 78, 85
mine (noun)   83
ministry   32, 74
miracles   19, 51, 58
Miriam   4, 39
money   8, 44, 55, 77
morning 12, 33, 49, 54, 81, 85, 86, 97
Moses   4, 5, 6, 39, 61
Mottingham   87–90
Mount of Olives (hill) 58
mountain(s)6, 23, 36, 63, 74, 93

music   26, 52, 84, 89, 94, 98, 99

names/titles of God 6, 7, 15, 20, 23, 27, 28, 80, 92
names/titles of Jesus   3, 42, 44, 46, 48, 52, 53, 58, 60–62, 67, 73, 80, 81, 86, 89, 91, 92
Naomi   39
Nathanael   47
nations   8, 21, 23, 33, 70, 80, 81, 91, App 2
Nazareth   56, 58, 91
Nehemiah   39
neighbours   7, 25, 56, 64, 93, 99
new birth   56, 68, 97, App 2
new creation   35, 75, 81
new year   41, 78
Nile   39
Noah   39

old age   4, 24, 35, 36

palaces   66
parables   14, 25, 43, 44, 82
Paradise   39
parents   7, 39, 52, 53, 87, 89, 90
Passover   61
Paul   94
Peckham   93, 94
Pentecost   35, 36, 84, 94
Peter   47, 69, 94, 96
Pharaoh   21
Philip (apostle)   47
Philip (deacon)   94
Pilgrim Homes   4, 24, 99
pilgrims, pilgrimage   4, 16, 53, 65, 74, 87, 98

prison   17, 33, 49, 69, 82, 94
prophets, prophecy   4, 23–39, 42, 58, 71, 95
proverbs   10
Psalm(s)   12–21

Rahab   39
rain   21, 36
Reading (Berks)   83
reconciliation   38, 70, 71
redemption, Redeemer   19, 20, 83, 85, 100
repentance   31, 32, 40, 42, 49, 70, 71, 96
rest   8, 15, 59, 88, 99, App 2
riches, see money, wealth
river(s)   30, 32, 39, 42, 54, 58, 95
Rochester   95
rule of God   1, 19, 25, 29, 33, 76, 96
Ruth   39

Sabbath   7, 59, 88, 99
Sacraments   94
Samaritans (NT)   94
Samson   39
Samuel   39
Sarah   4, 39
Saul   39
school(s)   8, 25, 74, 87–90, 98
science   2, 89, 98
Scribe   12, 39
Scripture(s)   4, 12, 31, 39, 46, 58, 61, 74, 82, 83, 89, 91, 94–96, 100
Scotland   88
sea   21, 37, 39, 89, 96
seraphim   46

sharing, co-operation, teamwork   22, 25, 89, 90, 93, 98
shepherds   9, 86, 94, 96
silence   50, 51, 89, 99
Simeon   4, 94
Simon (Zelotes)   47
slavery, slaves   1, 5, 15, 71, 100, App 2
soldiers   50, 91
Solomon   10, 11, 39, 61
sport   88, 90, 98
stone(s)   9, 17, 49, 89, 97, 98, App 2
Streatham   100
study   74

teaching   12, 23, 32, 74, 80, 96
tears   12, 17, 25, 29, 36, 52, 88, 91
temple   10, 82
Ten Commandments   7
Thaddaeus   47
thanksgiving   24, 38, 70, 75, 83, 87, 95
thieves, stealing   7, 15, 62
Thomas   47
time, times   8, 16, 17, 29, 30, 34, 35, 39–41, 48, 49, 56, 68, 74, 83, 87, 90, 92, 94, 98, 99
transfiguration   50
travelling, journeys   4–6, 26, 37, 39, 40, 51, 53, 58, 65, 74, 83, 87, 93, 94
treasure   10, 14, 43, 44, 66
tree (cross)   16, 50, 57, 58
trees   2, 10, 13, 39, 48, 87, 89
Trinity   74, 80, 85, 94

trumpets 36, 80	washing feet 63	work, human 7, 18, 22,
twelve disciples 22, 47	water(s) 5, 13, 49,	25, 27, 39, 42, 51, 63,
tyranny, tyrants 5, 30,	51, 56, 61, 97	65, 70, 82, 89, 90, 95, 96
33, 38	wealth 10, 11, 14, 15,	
	18, 37, 43, 44, 66, 77, 83	years 16, 39, 41, 49, 74,
unity 70, 71, 99	West Smethwick 84	84, 90, 95, 99, 100
upper room 16, 49	wine 26, 36, 51	youth 25, 35, 36
	wisdom, wise 10, 11,	
visions 28–30, 32, 35	19, 34, 61, 78, 83, 84	Zacchaeus 55, 94
	word(s) of God 12, 14,	Zechariah (OT) 39
Walworth 91–92	29, 40, 43, 74, 83, 85	Zechariah (NT) 4
war and peace 8, 23, 33,	work, divine 50, 54,	Zion 4, 12, 17, 21
70, 71, 79, 88, 95	59, 93, App 2	

INDEX OF TUNES

A WORLD OF OUR OWN 39	DARWALL'S 148th 77	HIMLEY 84
ALLELUIA (Wesley) 51	DIX 12, 47	HOPE REVIVED 68
AMAZING GRACE (NEW BRITAIN) 100	DOWN AT THE STATION 64	INCARNATION 51
AN ENGLISH COUNTRY GARDEN 60	DUNFERMLINE 1	INTERCESSOR 17
ARGUMENTUM 79	ELLACOMBE 96	JERUSALEM 81
BATTLE HYMN OF THE REPUBLIC 54	ENGLAND'S LANE 13	JOEL 36
BISHOP JUSTUS 98	FABRE 2	JOHN BROWN'S BODY 54
BLACKBURN 23	FAIRMILE 5	KELVINGROVE 25
BONNYTON 1	FATHER I PLACE INTO YOUR HANDS 40	KERVAN COVE 63
BOWERHAM 57	FEN MEADOW 78	KING JESUS HATH A GARDEN 46
BUCKLAND 99	FINISHED 67	KINGSFOLD 24
BUNESSAN 6	FLOREAS FETTESIA 21	KOINONIA 71
CAMBERWELL 93	FORTY ACRES 62	LAMBERHURST 95
CEDARS 10	FULDA 73	LAUS DEO 74
CELESTE App 1	GIVE ME OIL IN MY LAMP 9	LEVAMENTUM 8
COME AND TASTE ALONG WITH ME 80	GRANDCHILDREN 92	LONDON NEW 1
CONTEMPLATION 83	GYLCOTE 92	LONDON'S BURNING 69
CROFTON LANE 20	HANOVER 28	LORD OF THE YEARS 35
CRÜGER 30	HEER JESUS HEEFT EEN HOFKEN 46	LÜBECK 99
DARETOBE 27	HESWALL 85	LUCKINGTON 90
	HILARITER 68	MAGDA 63

MARY'S BOY CHILD 31
NATIVITY   App 2
NEWINGTON   72
NEWSTEAD WOOD 86
O QUANTA QUALIA 34
ODE TO JOY   87
OLD YEAVERING   26
OTFORD   52
PACHELBEL   78
PEMBROKE   18
PORRESHA   78
PORTSMOUTH   97
PRECIOUS LORD,
   TAKE MY HAND 44
REPTON   4
ROCKINGHAM   79
ST BOTOLPH   83
ST COLUMBA   15
ST DENIO   3, 62
ST EDMUND   99

ST FULBERT   96
ST MARGARET   91
ST STEPHEN   42, 100
SALZBURG   99
SANS DAY CAROL 56
SEEK YE FIRST THE
   KINGDOM   14
SHAKER TUNE   58
SKIP TO MY LOU   43
SOLOMON   10
SONG 34   53, 89
SONG OF FAITH   65
STREETS OF LAREDO
                11, 45
STRENGTH AND STAY
                    17
STUTTGART   74
THE HOLLY AND THE
   IVY   41
THERE'S NOT A

FRIEND   76
THIS OLD MAN   22
TRURO   37, 88
TWINKLE, TWINKLE,
   LITTLE STAR   47
TWO THOUSAND
   YEARS   41
TYDI A RODDAIST 18
UNIVERSITY
   COLLEGE   5
VICTOR'S CROWN 48
VULPIUS   19
WAREHAM   16
WAS LEBET   32, 94
WHEN JESUS CAME 56
WINCHESTER NEW 82
WOLVERCOTE   49
WOODLEA   68
ZACCHAEUS   55

INDEX OF CONTEMPORARY COMPOSERS

Barnard, John   95
Baughen, Michael   35
Booker, Michael   78
Bryan, Paul   51
Canham, Jenny   57
Constable, Doug   78
Crothers, John   2, 63
Gilmurray, Sue 8, 71, 79

Gooch, Jonathan   68
Greenidge, Anne 10, 65,
                       98
Hayward, Christopher
10, 23, 27, 36, 41, 56, 67
Jones, William O   84
Low, Trevor   68
Mawson, Linda 20, 85, 86

Peacock, David   5
Raynor, Brian   51, 52
Tredinnick, Noël 26, 48
White, David Ashley 62
Wigmore, Paul   92
Woodcraft, Ruth   92

INDEX OF HYMN TEXTS

Number

All baptized beneath the cloud 72
All creation, sing to your rightful King 91
All things in Jesus were first created 76
As Jesus rested at the well 59
As special days adorn the year 16
At many times, in various ways 29

Beyond the street, the glory 97
Blessed, each one who does not walk 13

Christ, grant me grace to let you
    wash my feet 63
Come with us to sing new songs 98
Crossing the desert near the
    great mountain 6

Daniel the prophet bowed in prayer 31
Day of the Lord, how shall we know your
    coming 35
Dearer than gold are the
    words of the Lord 14

Father of one human race 80
Father, Saviour, Holy Spirit 74
Find rest, my soul, in God alone 15
Following Jesus one by one 47
For you and for many,
    the promise was spoken 45
From the water comes the child 5

Give glory to God for
    this busy half-century 94
Give thanks that God, the changeless One 38
God, loving ruler of our world 1
God of fresh discoveries 99
God says, 'I saved you, set you free' 7
God the I AM who does not change 92
Good Shepherd, you know us, you call us by
    name 62

Has nothing changed tonight 52
Have you heard of a lad called David 9
He walked by the river
    where the crowds had gone 58
Hear, you heavens, and listen, earth 23
Here I am, all alone 22
Here's what the kingdom of God is like 43
His name is Solomon 10
How wickedly they spread their lies 18

I am the bread, the bread of life 60
If conscience counts for more than might 79
If this is not our world 77
In exile from their homes 27
In the heartbeat of the city 26
In the public square they meet 12
Is the city all they say it is 25
It is the Lord who sends the storm 37
It's about time and years that count 40

Jesus commands us, 'Love one another' 64
Jordan is the shining river 54

Like a pearl of great price is the
    kingdom of God 44
Listening child of God 48
Long before Abraham 61
'Look unto me and be ye saved' App 2
Lord, hear my prayer! My cry shall
    come before you 17
Lord Jesus Christ, if day or night 24
Lord of Good News, as once you came 95

Mary of the incarnation 51

News from the south and the north 33
No stone left on another 49
Not even Adam gave a name 2
Not so very far 67

O Adam, our Adam, the very first man 3
O Christ, the Son of God Most High 73
O praise the Lord; proclaimed, adored 20
On Jordan's river bank today 42
One hundred years are ours to celebrate 90
One in Christ – and must
    we fight each other 70
One small landmark set in London 87
Our Jesus has a kingdom
    that is open wide 46

Ring those bells! This year, every year 85

Simon Peter was arrested 69
Since first we joined the pilgrim way 4
Sing once again, God's name be praised 21
So shall the land have rest from war 8
So this is the day when his
    God does not answer 50
Soon comes the time of
    the archangel Michael 34

Thanks be to God for his
    grace beyond speech 75
That evening in the Friday gloom 68
That year they laid one royal stone 89
The ancient hills have known his word 82
The feet of God have touched this earth 57
The Lord once gave the vision 30
The morning comes:
    new heavens, new earth 81

The place took its name from a skull App 1
The powers of kings,
    their robes and rings 66
The prophet speaks, the locusts come 36
They came to hear the word of God 96
This is the man who runs with God 88
Two hundred years have passed 84
Two thousand years of sorrow 41

We are one in Christ and
    can never be at war 71
We have not walked these paths before 78
We take our silver from the mine 83
Welcome to the wedding 93
What Daniel has seen in visions by night 28
What did you know, small unborn God 53
When Abraham at seventy-five 100
When glory shone through the dark skies 86
When Jesus came to Bethlehem 56
When Solomon came to be
    king of all Israel 11
When the Lord made the
    earth by his loving plan 39
When we encounter
    the wonder of prophecy 32
With all my heart I praise the Lord 19

Yes, this is the way for us to walk 65

Zacchaeus was a very little man / walked a
    very little way 55

HOLY WEEK, CLOSE UP

He washed the feet of Simon
who did not wish it so;
he dried them with a towel,
though Simon had said no.

He washed the feet of Andrew;
if Andrew spoke at all
we do not have his comments.

He washed the feet of Thomas;
his fingers probed the skin.

He washed the feet of Judas.

EASTER, FROM A DISTANCE

I would not make too much a fist
of being a signed-up atheist,
with all the things I'd have to change
and all the days to rearrange,
dismiss religion as a bore
and just not bother any more.
Yes, I have given it some thought;
the trouble is, I might be caught
stealing a glance as sunset came
with every cloud a crimson flame,
or standing near some waterfall
stunned by the glory of it all.
They might spy out my furtive look
inside some shrewd and dusty book
or, coming in a bit too soon,
might hear me try out some new tune,
or mention heaven, or breathe a prayer
as if my Father were still there.
I might be stirred to fresh surprise
to see the way a Christian dies,
or sometimes, to my secret shame,
still taste the sweetness of that Name.
Or I might wonder at his words,
or see the stars, or hear the birds,
or find a beetle in the wood
or think of nails and thorns and blood.
Or maybe, even, God might see
this furtive, hunted creature (me),
as it slipped in behind the arch
of some forgotten little church
where I had quietly crept inside
to hear 'This joyful Eastertide'.